Joachim Klang

TIPS FOR KIDS MINIONS

COOL PROJECTS FOR YOUR LEGO® BOX

HEEL

THANKS

To pioneers and revolutionaries, some of whom I know personally and admire.

2LegoOrNot2Lego
Arvo Brothers
ArzLan
Bart Willen
Brian Corredor
Bricksonwheels
Brickthing
Bricktrix
Bruceywan
captainsmog
Cole Blaq
Cuahchic
DecoJim
- Derfel Cadarn -
Digger1221
Eastpole77
Fianat
Fraslund
Fredoichi
Gabe Umland
Gambort
gearcs
Henrik Hoexbroe
Homa
Joe Meno
Jojo
Karwik
Lazer Blade
lego_nabii
Legohaulic
LEGOLAS
Legonardo Davidy
Legopard
Legotrucks
lichtblau
‚LL'
Mark of Falworth
markus19840420
marshal banana
McBricker
Mijasper
Misterzumbi
Nannan Z
NENN
Obedient Machine
Ochre Jelly
„Orion Pax"
Paul Vermeesch
Pepa Quin
RoccoB
Sir Nadroj
Sirens-Of-Titan
Spencer_R
T.Oechsner
Taz-Maniac
ted @ndes
TheBrickAvenger
Théolego
tnickolaus
Toltomeja
x_Speed
Xenomurphy

Particular thanks are due to my coauthors, Uwe Kurth, who has even been known to shake a few trees out of his sleeves in his sleep, and Lutz Uhlmann, as always, for digitizing my constructions.

Special thanks also go to German-Brick-Circus for his tremendous support.

HEEL Verlag GmbH
Gut Pottscheidt
53639 Königswinter
Germany
Tel.: +49(0)2223 9230-0
Fax: +49(0)2223 9230-13
E-Mail: info@heel-verlag.de
www.heel-verlag.de

Author: Joachim Klang
Layout, Design, and Illustration: Odenthal Illustration, www.odenthal-illustration.de
Photography: Thomas Schultze, www.thomas-schultze.de
Translated from German by: Laila Friese in association with First Edition Translations Ltd, Cambridge, UK
Edited by: Robert Anderson in association with First Edition Translations Ltd, Cambridge, UK
Project management: Ulrike Reihn-Hamburger

Printed in Hungary

ISBN 978-3-95843-494-3

CONTENT

PREFACE

A vast world of colorful bricks—that is surely an apt description for the variety and choice you get with LEGO® pieces. Anyway, who can say that they have already seen and tried everything? There is always something new to discover, just as there is in every LEGO® collector's box.

As always, I started to think about the models I could build for this book without first thinking about which bricks I would need. In the end, the list of models was longer than the scope of this book, of course, and sometimes I didn't have some of the bricks I needed for my ideas. So either I had to come up with an alternative or go and get the bricks.

It will be the same for you when you try to make these models. Unfortunately, I can only guess which bricks you are likely to have in your box, as this depends on the sets you already possess. This is why I have tried to build each model to match the original as closely as possible. That's the challenge!

You should, however, make your own decisions about how closely you want to follow my ideas or whether you want to make your own versions. Have you got all the pieces? Do you want to get the missing bricks? Or would you rather make do with what you have? Everyone will have different ideas about the details they think are important, won't they? My personal aim, however, is to show you what I think gets the best results—but, of course, it's fine to do something different.

Think like this: Perhaps one of your friends has a spare one of the piece missing from your collection? Maybe you can get it in a small set in a local store? You could also order it on the Internet, for example on eBay or at BrickLink. Or get it at LEGOLAND®, the LEGO® Store, or the LEGO® Online shop. You might even get lucky at a flea market or at a LEGO® BrickSwap.

In the end, there is just one person who has to be content with the finished model—the builder. It doesn't have to look 100 percent like my original. For my Gru mobile, for example, I looked around for templates on the Internet and found many LEGO® creations. You can use these templates, too, if you want.

The main thing is to have fun! I have a lot of fun seeing my models grow. Often, I only come up with different, simpler, or better ways of doing things a while after I've finished my first attempt. I even came up with more ideas after we'd taken all the photos! I bet you will do the same.

After all, it's all about creativity! That's exactly why Ole Kirk Christiansen invented these plastic bricks in 1949.

Joe

USING A MINIFIGURE SCALE FOR MINIONS

It isn't easy to build minions on a minifigure scale with the currently available range of LEGO® bricks. You can see my results here. I've had to build our little yellow friends "on their heads," so to speak, because I naturally wanted to have the round blue block at the bottom. With simple, round, 2x2 plates you can change the size of the figure at will.

MINION

As I said in the preface, you sometimes get an idea after you've already finished something. For example, take this Minion here—I already had a construction guide for it in my book „Tips, tricks and building techniques for LEGO® bricks". Later, I thought of a simpler construction and so I'm happy to present it here now. You don't need any special instructions for the different facial expressions that you will see in the next few pages. Just take a closer look at them.

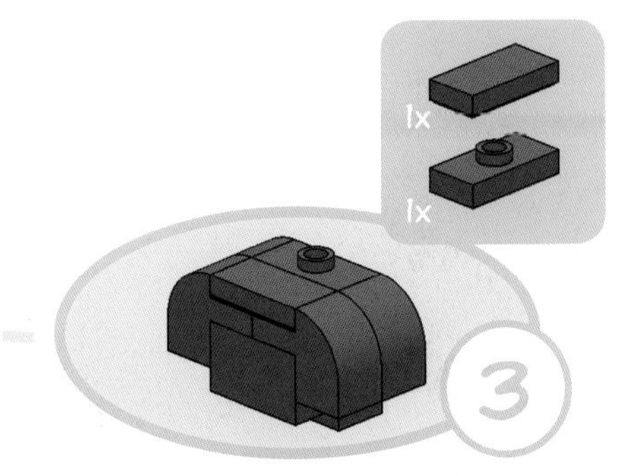

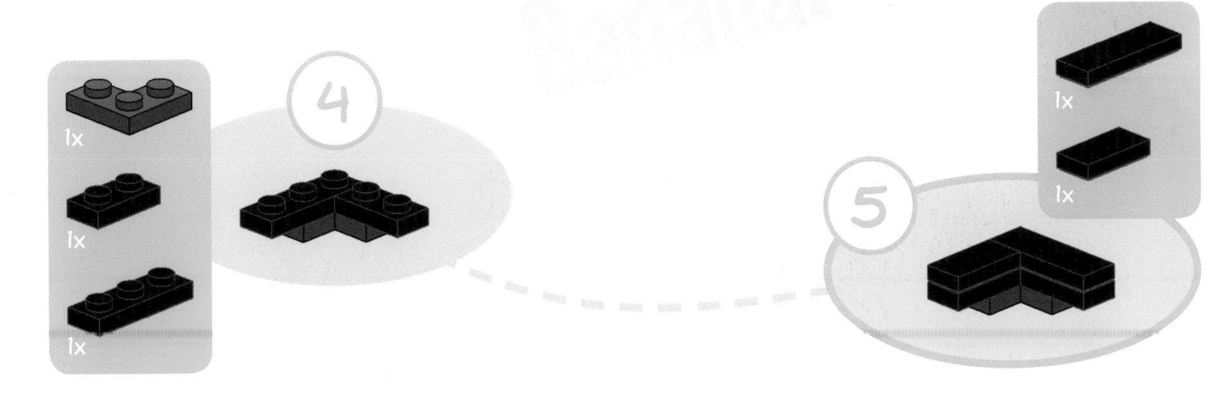

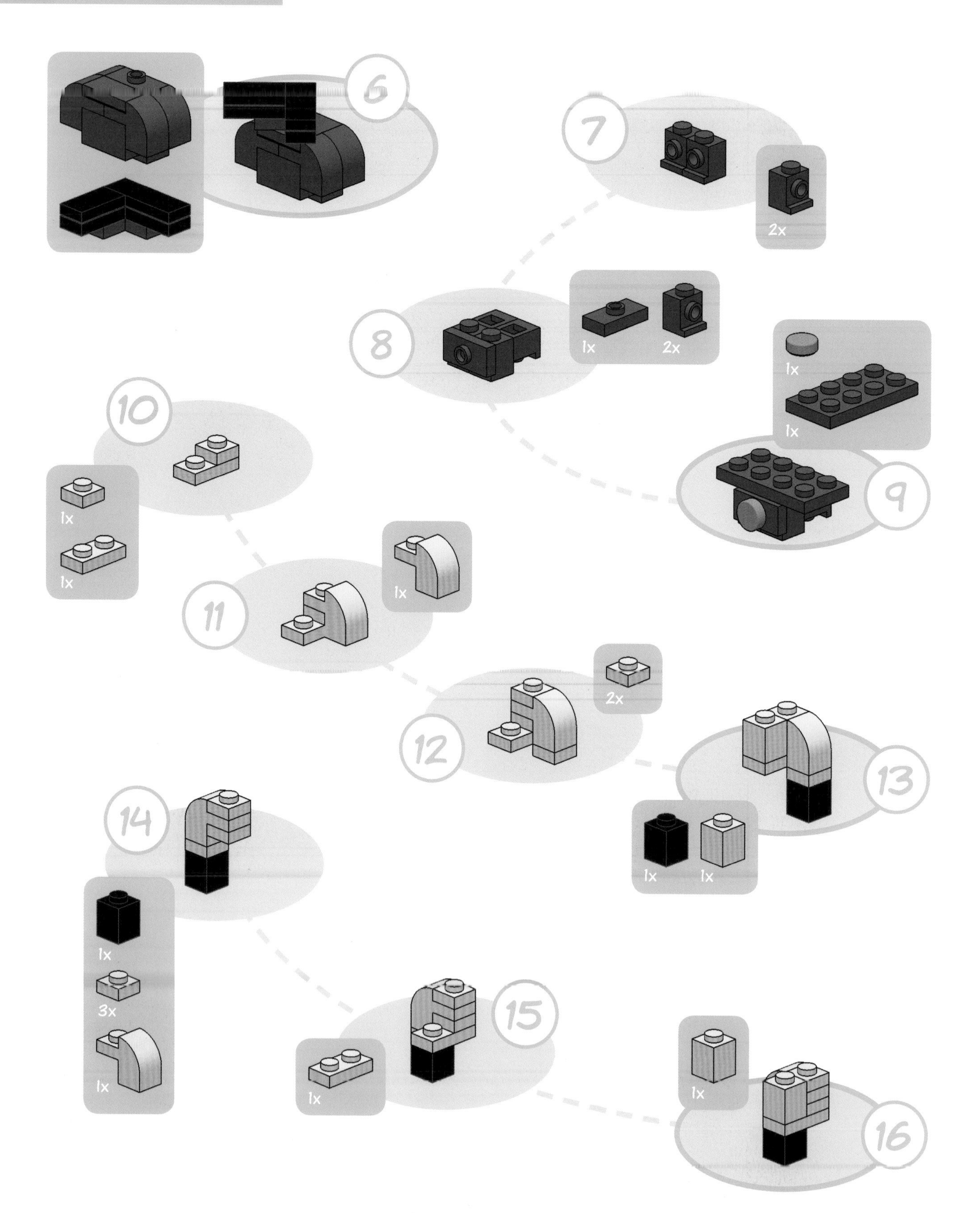
6
7
2x
8
1x
2x
1x
1x
9
10
1x
1x
11
1x
12
2x
13
1x
1x
14
1x
3x
1x
15
1x
16
1x

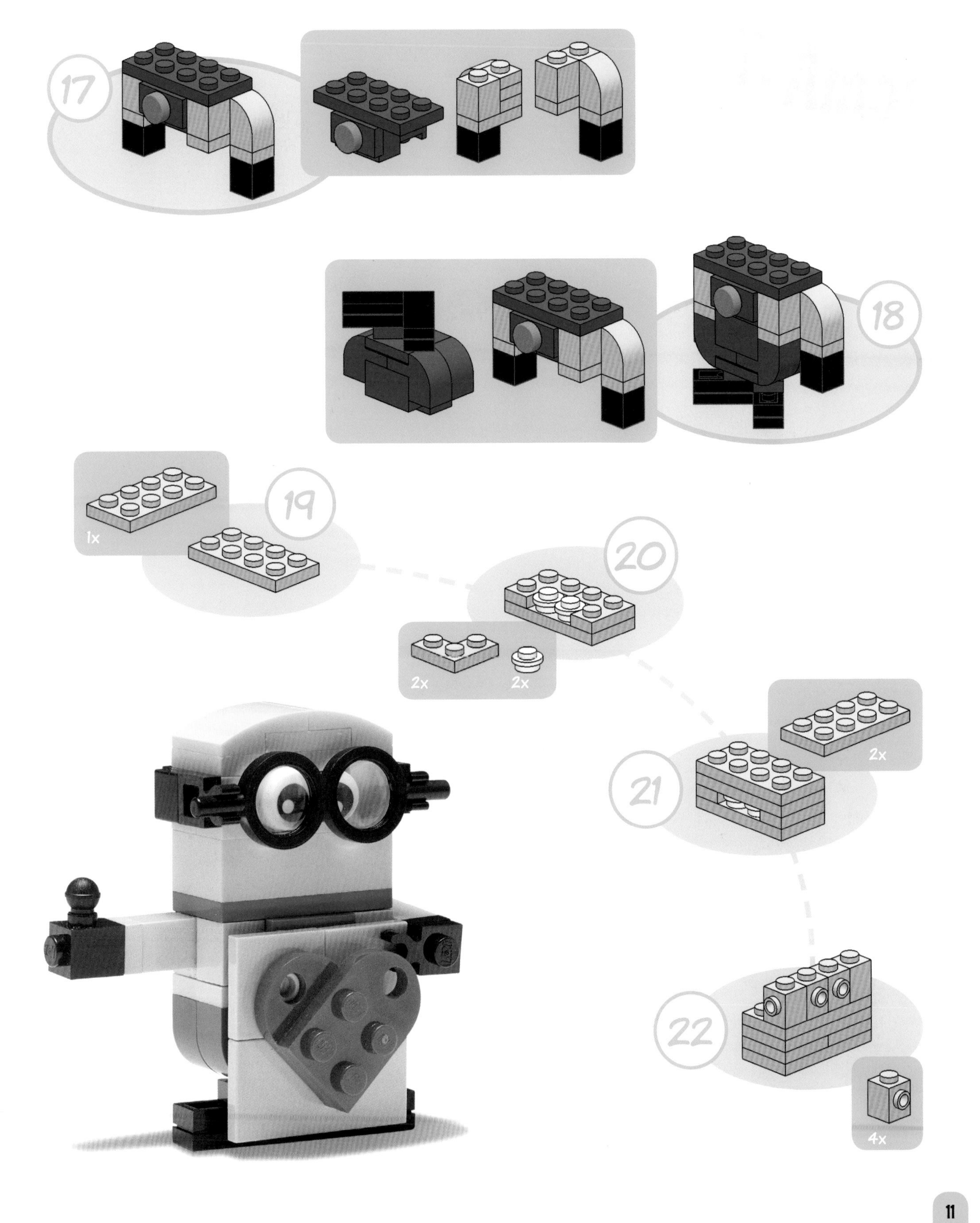
17
18
1x
19
20
2x
2x
21
2x
22
4x

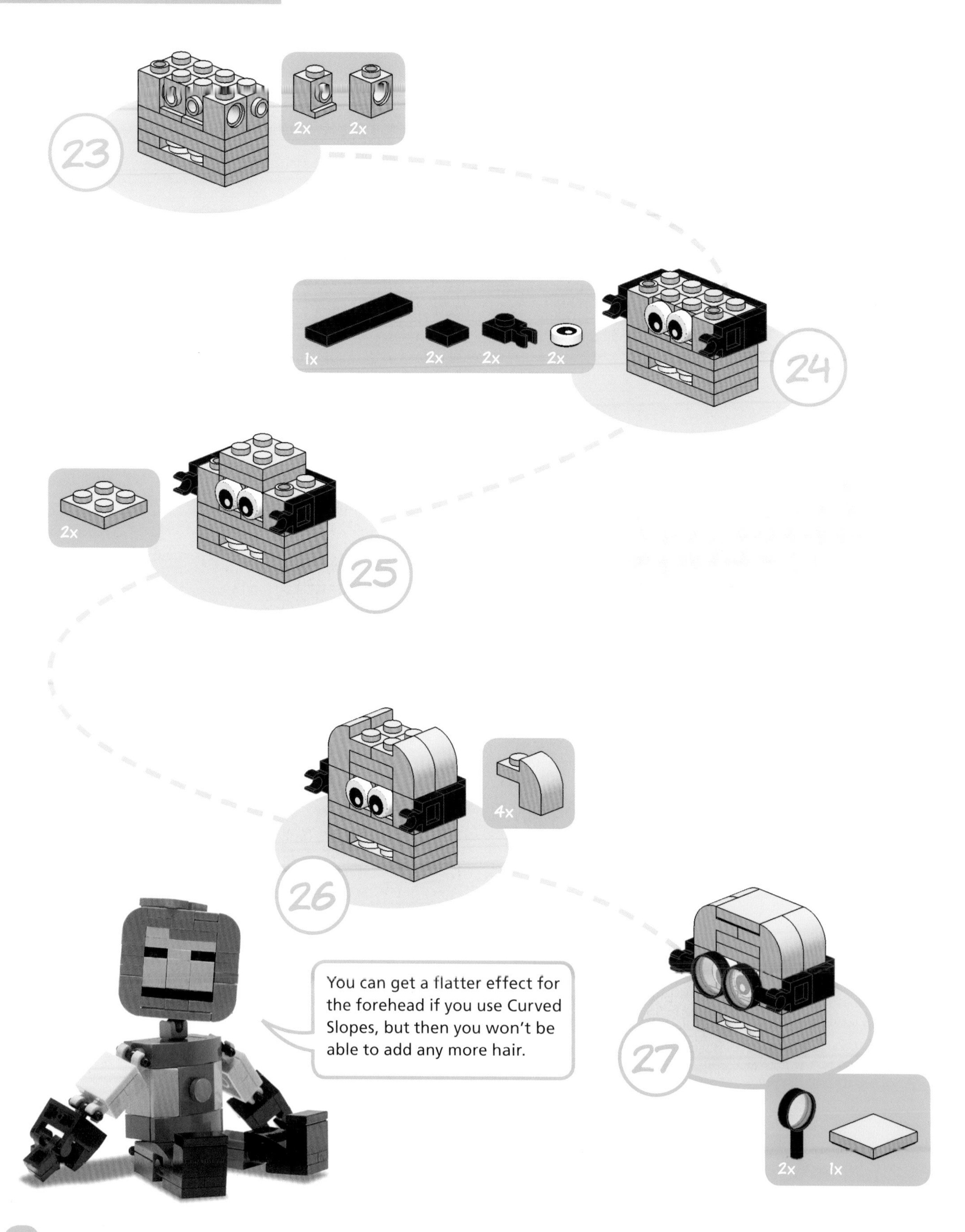
23
2x
2x
1x
2x
2x
2x
24
2x
25
4x
26
You can get a flatter effect for the forehead if you use Curved Slopes, but then you won't be able to add any more hair.
27
2x
1x

28

PARTS LIST

Quantity	Color	Element	Element Name	LEGO® Number
2	Black	3005	Brick 1 x 1	300526
2	Yellow	3005	Brick 1 x 1	300524
4	Blue	4070	Brick 1 x 1 with Headlight	407023
2	Yellow	4070	Brick 1 x 1 with Headlight	407024
4	Yellow	87087	Brick 1 x 1 with Stud on 1 Side	4624985
4	Blue	6091	Brick 2 x 1 x 1 & 1/3 with Curved Top	4189123, 4519981, 609123
6	Yellow	6091	Brick 2 x 1 x 1 & 1/3 with Curved Top	4160863, 4188357, 609124
1	Blue	3003	Brick 2 x 2	300323
2	Black	90463c01	Minifig Tool Magnifying Glass	4587893
6	Yellow	3024	Plate 1 x 1	302424
2	White	4073	Plate 1 x 1 Round	614101
2	Black	4085	Plate 1 x 1 with Clip Vertical Type 1	4617547, 4550017
1	Black	3023	Plate 1 x 2	302326
1	Blue	3023	Plate 1 x 2	302323
2	Yellow	3023	Plate 1 x 2	302324
2	Blue	3794	Plate 1 x 2 without Groove with 1 Centre Stud	379423
1	Black	3623	Plate 1 x 3	362326
2	Yellow	3022	Plate 2 x 2	302224, 4613978
1	Blue	2420	Plate 2 x 2 Corner	242023
2	Yellow	2420	Plate 2 x 2 Corner	242024
1	Blue	3020	Plate 2 x 4	302023
3	Yellow	3020	Plate 2 x 4	302024
2	Yellow	6541	Technic Brick 1 x 1 with Hole	654124
1	Flat Silver	98138	Tile 1 x 1 Round with Groove	4655241
2	Black	3070b	Tile 1 x 1 with Groove	307026
1	Black	3069b	Tile 1 x 2 with Groove	306926
1	Blue	3069b	Tile 1 x 2 with Groove	306926
1	Black	63864	Tile 1 x 3 with Groove	4558170
1	Black	2431	Tile 1 x 4 with Groove	243126
1	Yellow	3068b	Tile 2 x 2 with Groove	306824
2	White	98138p07	Tile Round 1 x 1 with Eye Pattern	6029156, 6001609

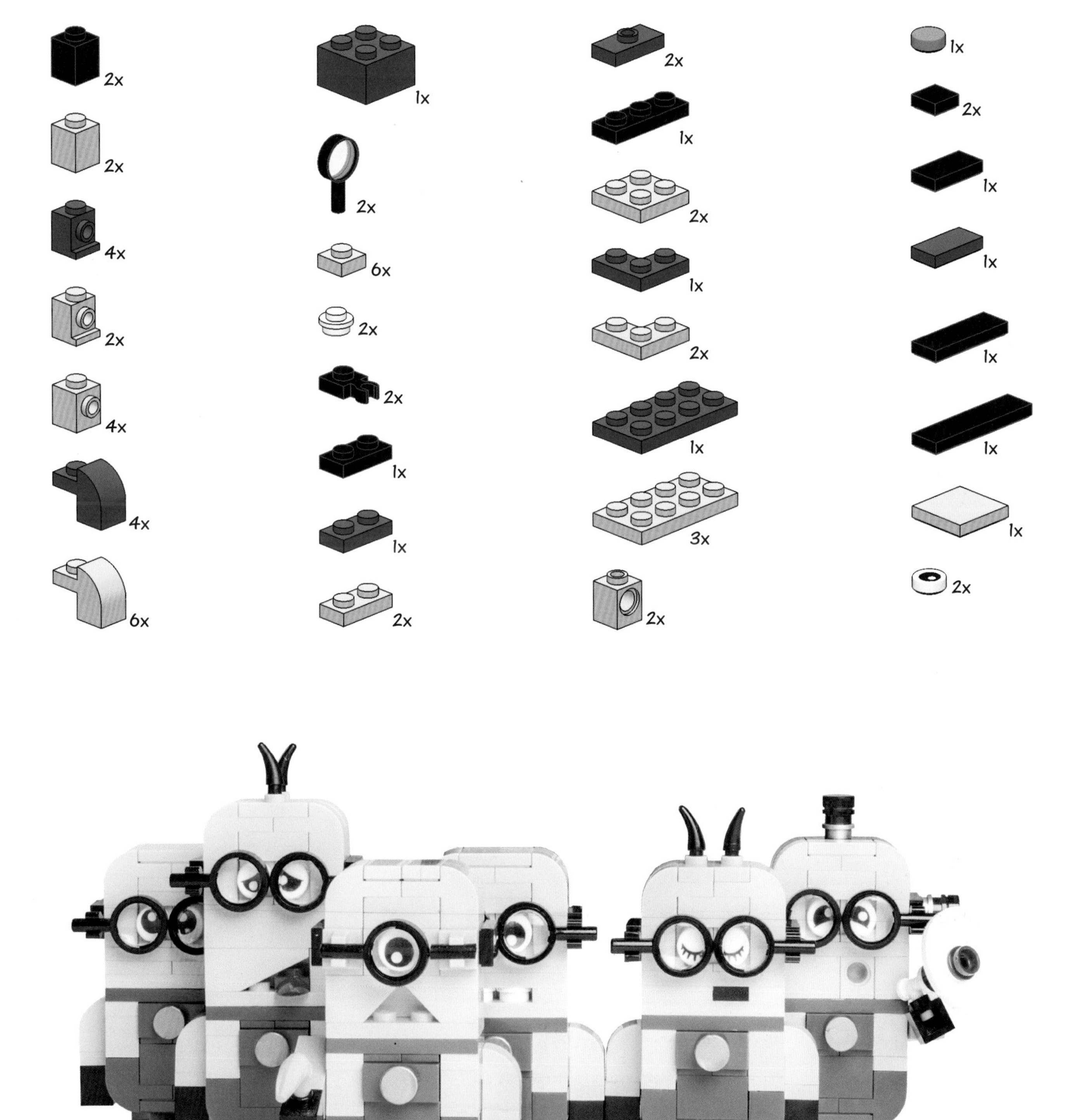
2x
2x
4x
2x
4x
4x
6x
1x
2x
6x
2x
2x
1x
1x
2x
2x
1x
2x
1x
2x
1x
3x
2x
1x
2x
1x
1x
1x
1x
1x
2x

HYDRANT „PAPAYA"

The core piece of the hydrant in miniature size is the 1x1 block with knobs on all four sides. Strangely, this brick has never been part of any set in yellow or red, but I have used it here since you can buy it on the Internet, for example. It is relatively expensive because it is rare, but you can also use it in a different color—it all depends on what you want.

ROCKET LAUNCHER

One of the most popular scenes of the first movie is the one with the rocket launcher during Gru's speech. This „Explosion photo" shows you my suggestion for a construction method.

EVIL MINION

In conversations with friends and acquaintances, I discovered that this funny fellow was quite well received. I was often asked how I had managed to get the hair right. Now I finally have the opportunity to explain it in detail.

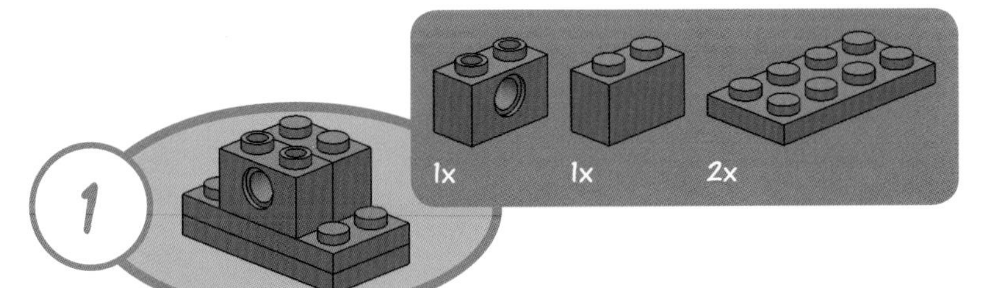

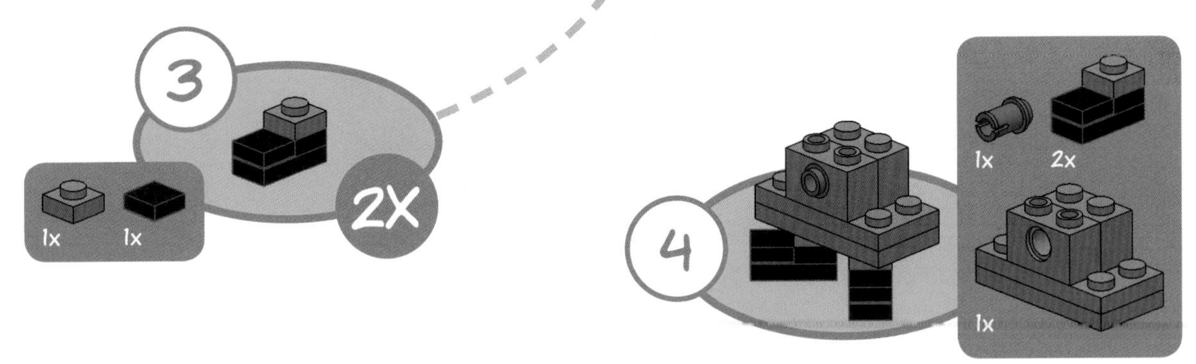

5
1x
1x
6
1x
1x
7
1x
1x
1x
8
1x
1x
9
1x
1x
10
1x
1x
1x
11
1x

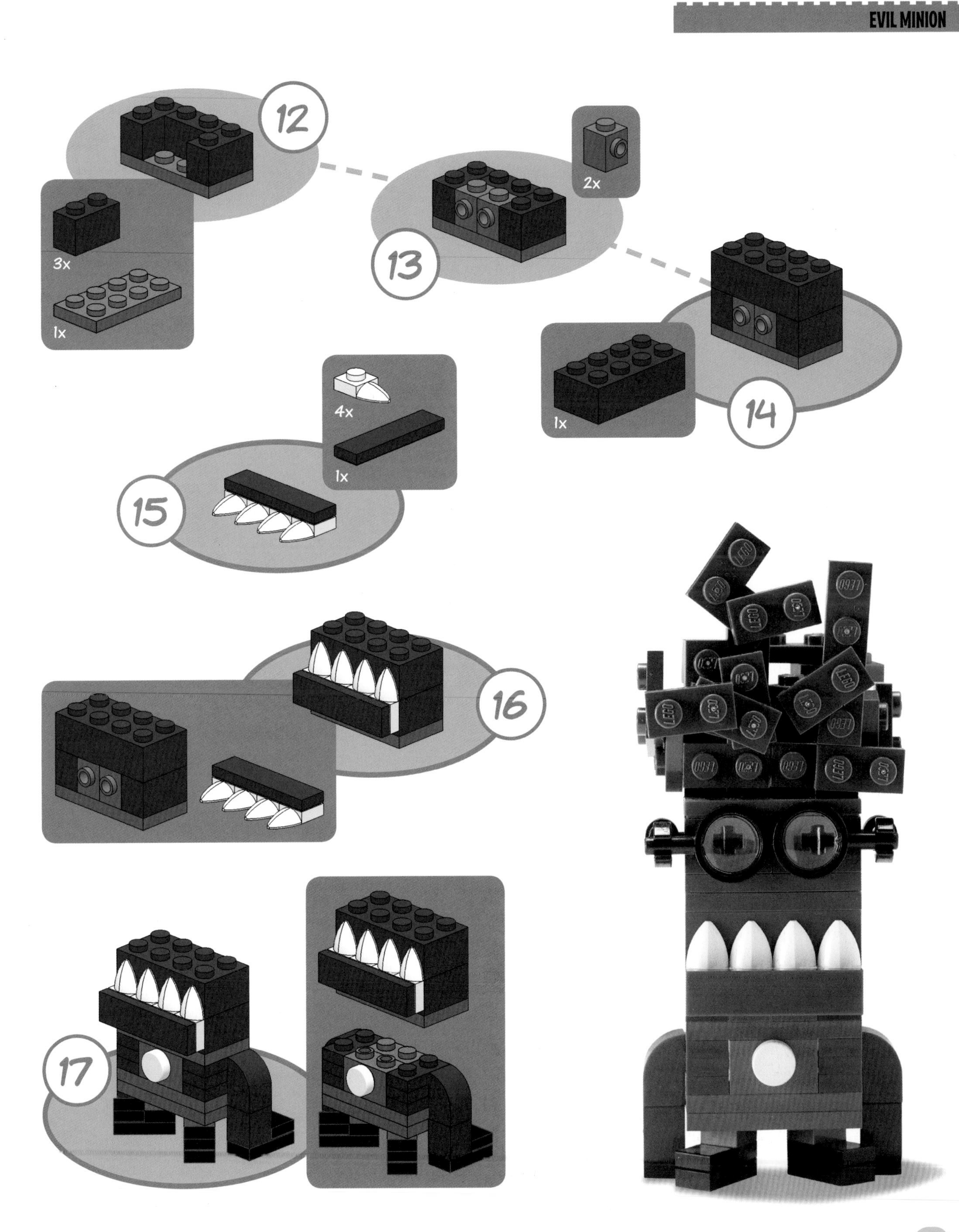
12
3x
1x
13
2x
14
1x
15
4x
1x
16
17

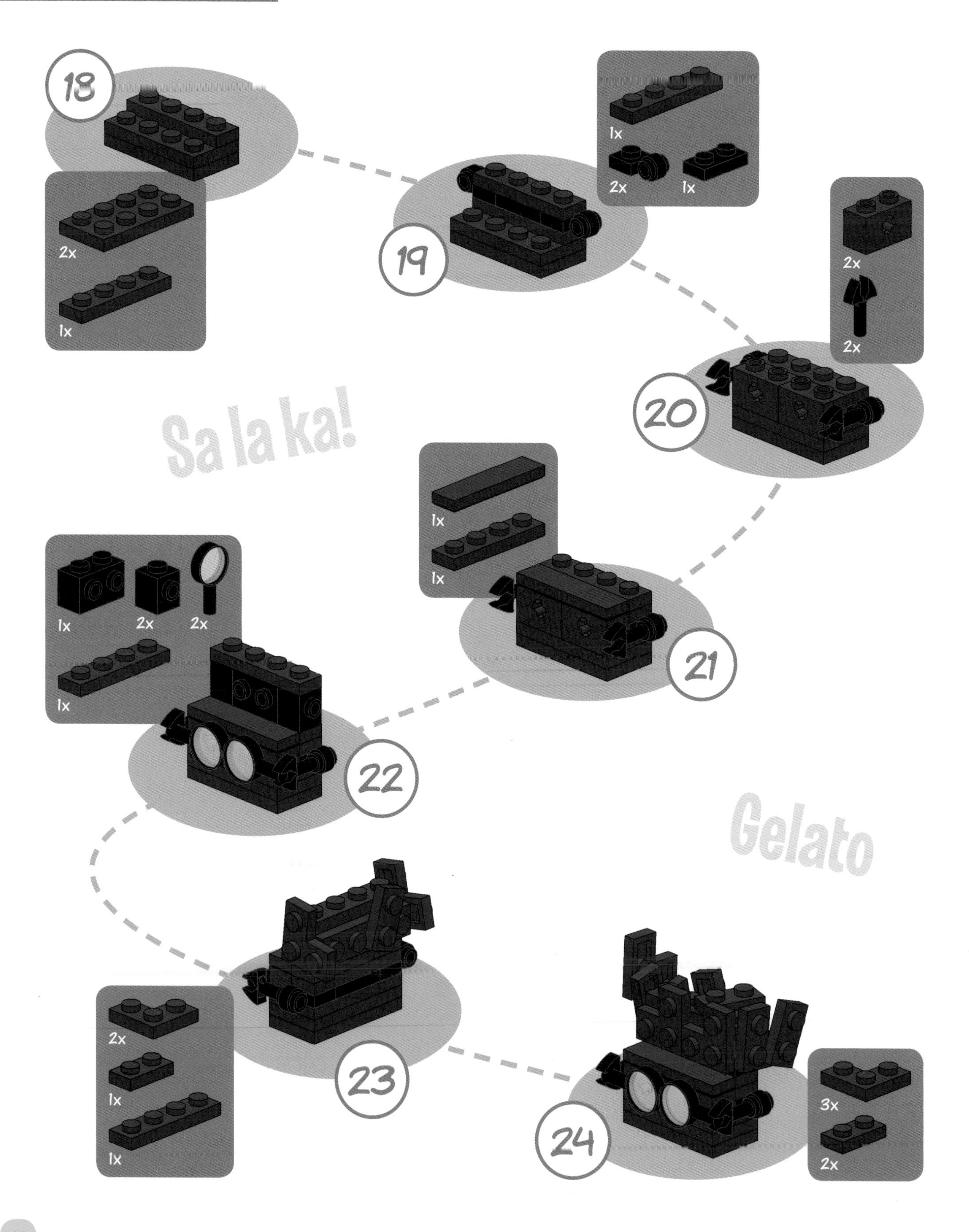
18
2x
1x
19
1x
2x
1x
20
2x
2x
Sa la ka!
1x
1x
21
1x
2x
2x
1x
22
Gelato
23
2x
1x
1x
24
3x
2x

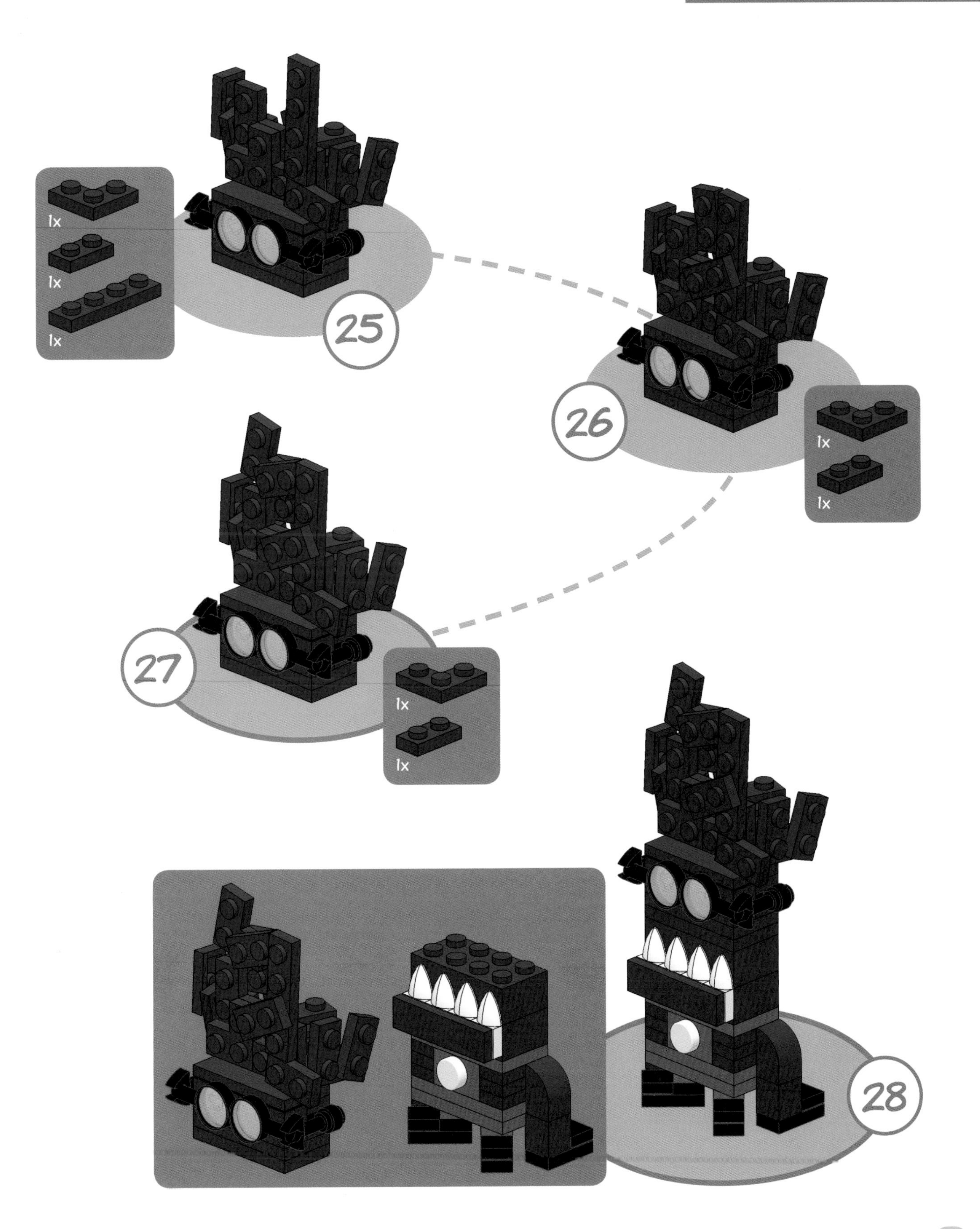
1x
1x
1x
25
26
1x
1x
27
1x
1x
28

PARTS LIST

Quantity	Color	Element	Element Name	LEGO® Number
2	Black	48729	Bar 1.5L with Clip	4289538
2	Dark Purple	3005	Brick 1 x 1	4224851, 4640738, 6084028
2	Black	87087	Brick 1 x 1 with Stud on 1 Side	4558954
2	Dark Bluish Gray	87087	Brick 1 x 1 with Stud on 1 Side	4558955
1	Dark Bluish Gray	3004	Brick 1 x 2	4211088
3	Dark Purple	3004	Brick 1 x 2	4224854, 4640739, 6104154
1	Black	52107	Brick 1 x 2 with Studs on Sides	4253815
2	Dark Purple	6091	Brick 2 x 1 x 1 & 1/3 with Curved Top	4224935, 4579032
1	Dark Purple	3001	Brick 2 x 4	4225243, 4626935
2	Black	90463c01	Minifig Tool Magnifying Glass	4587893
2	Black	3024	Plate 1 x 1	302426
2	Dark Bluish Gray	3024	Plate 1 x 1	4210719
2	Dark Purple	3024	Plate 1 x 1	4224857
2	Black	4081b	Plate 1 x 1 with Clip Light Type 2	408126, 4632571
4	White	49668	Plate 1 x 1 with Tooth	4224792
5	Black	3023	Plate 1 x 2	302326
10	Dark Purple	3023	Plate 1 x 2	4224858, 4655695
6	Dark Purple	3710	Plate 1 x 4	4225140
8	Dark Purple	2420	Plate 2 x 2 Corner	4225179
3	Dark Bluish Gray	3020	Plate 2 x 4	4211065
2	Dark Purple	3020	Plate 2 x 4	4224862
2	Dark Purple	32064b	Technic Brick 1 x 2 with Axlehole Type 2	4261363
1	Dark Bluish Gray	3700	Technic Brick 1 x 2 with Hole	4211111
1	Blue	4274	Technic Pin 1/2	4143005
1	White	98138	Tile 1 x 1 Round with Groove	4646844
4	Black	3070b	Tile 1 x 1 with Groove	307026
2	Dark Purple	2431	Tile 1 x 4 with Groove	4225185, 6057988

2x

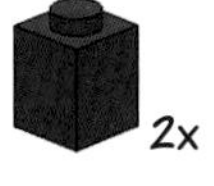
2x

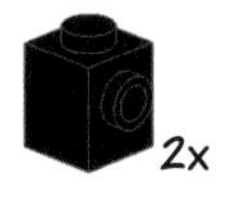
2x

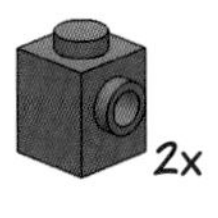
2x

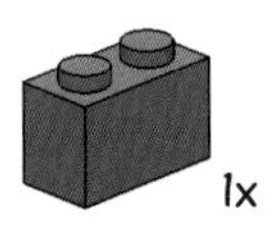
1x

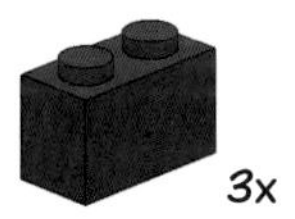
3x

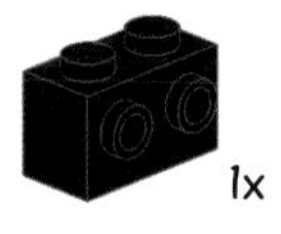
1x

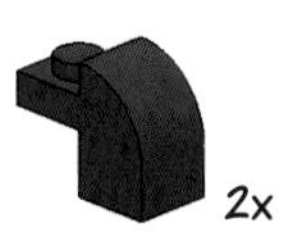
2x

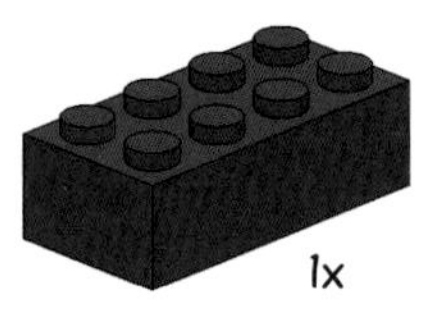
1x

2x

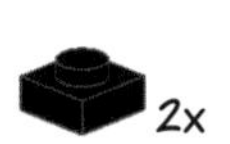
2x

2x

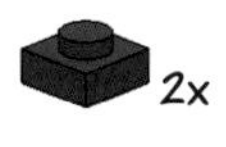
2x

2x

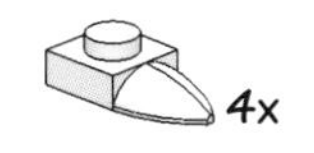
4x

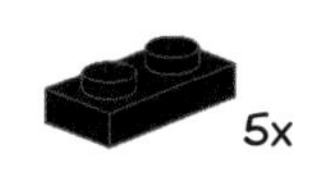
5x

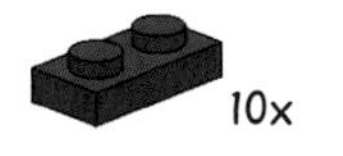
10x

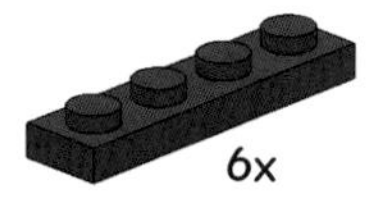
6x

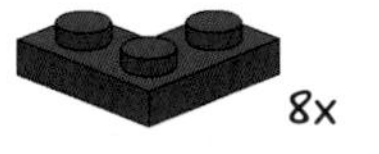
8x

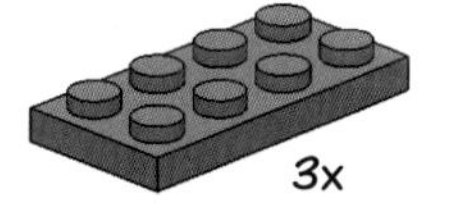
3x

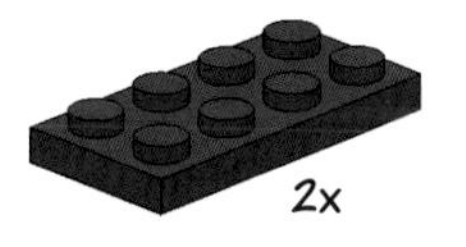
2x

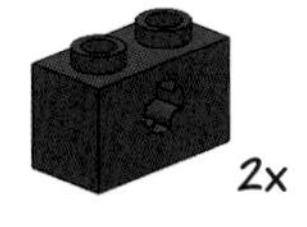
2x

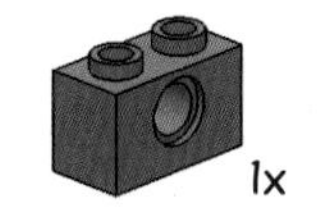
1x

1x

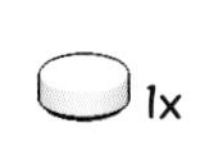
1x

4x

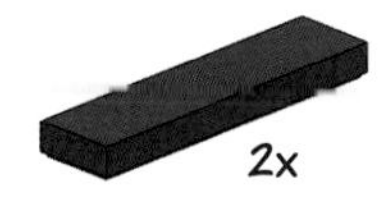
2x

FELONIUS GRU

We can't possibly leave out this likeable super-villain and Minions' employer. It is also possible to achieve a very high recognition value at this scale even with very common LEGO® bricks. My wife finds him so funny that he seems to have become a permanent fixture in our living room in the last few weeks. After the photo shoot, I made a few changes to the model so that Gru can also rotate his head.

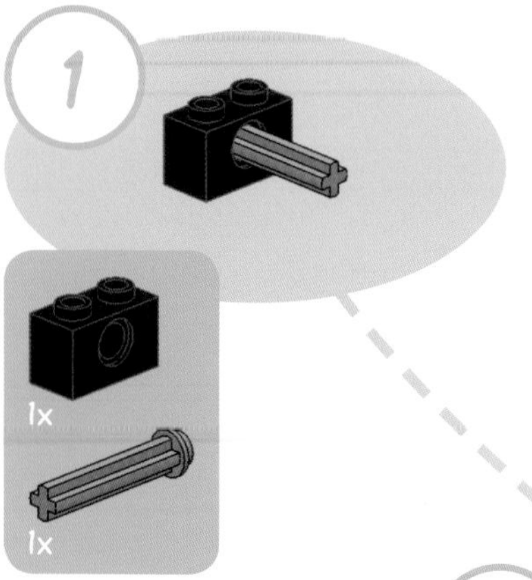

1

1x

1x

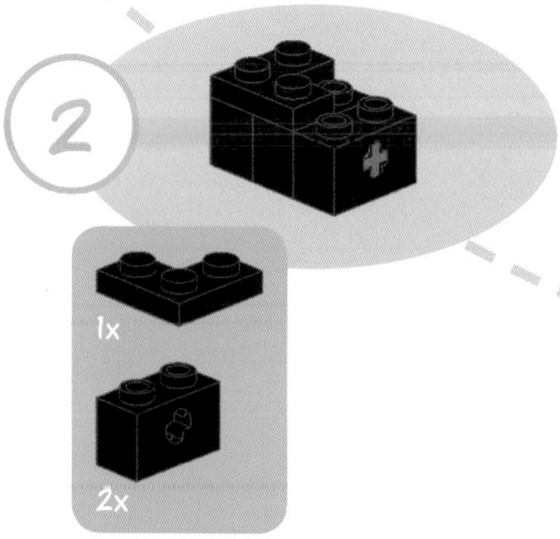

2

1x

2x

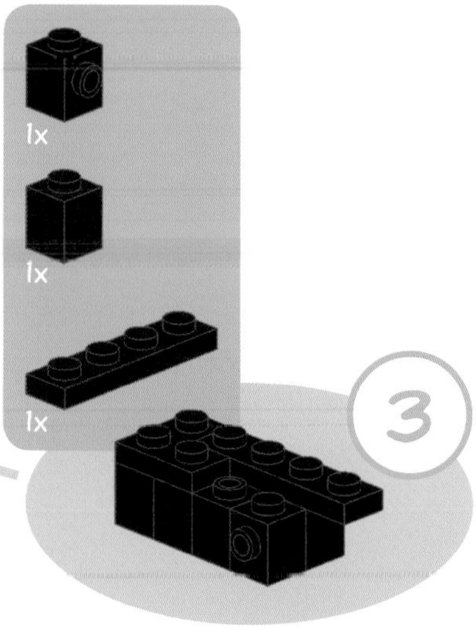

1x

1x

1x

3

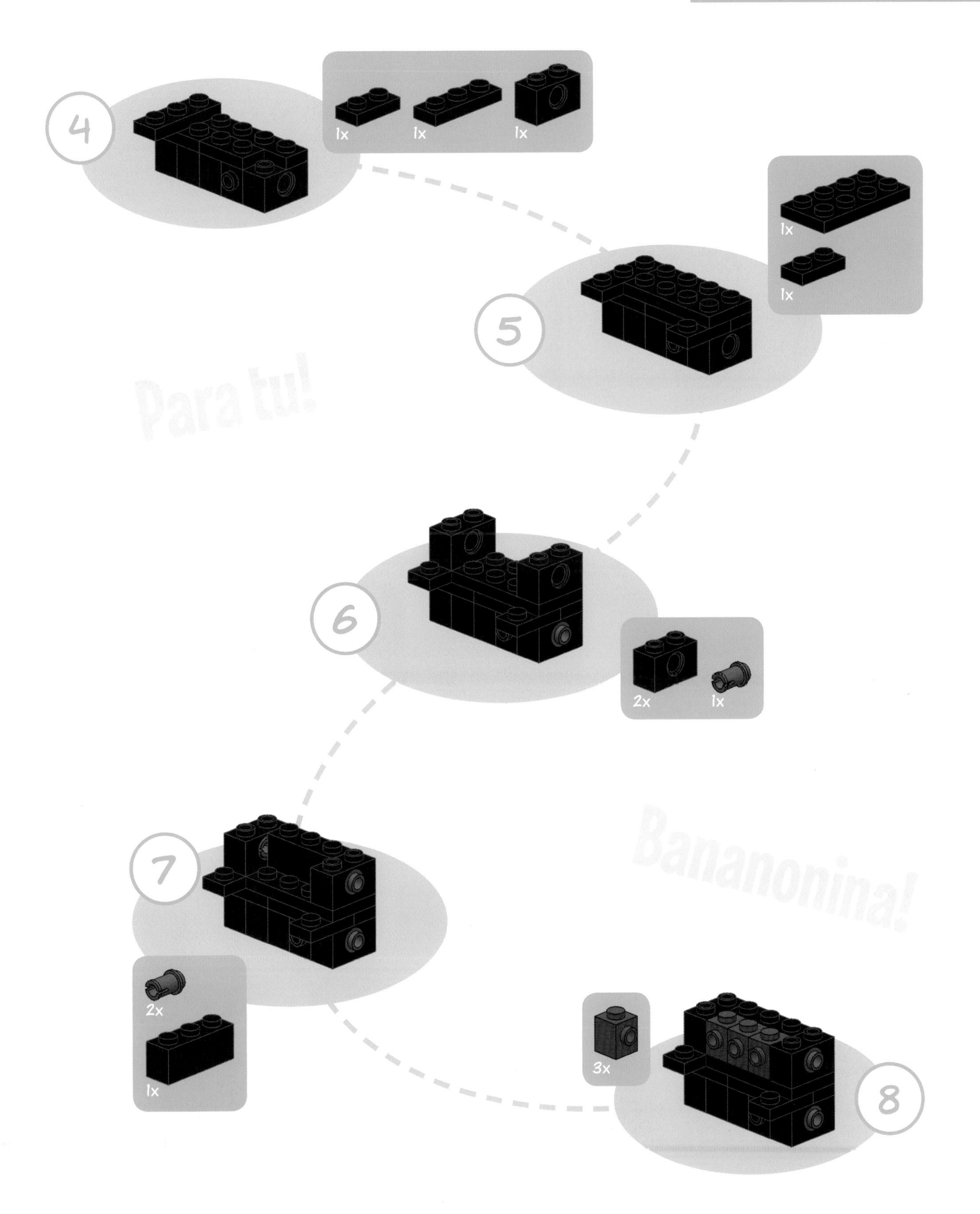
4
1x
1x
1x
5
1x
1x
Para tu!
6
2x
1x
7
2x
1x
Bananonina!
3x
8

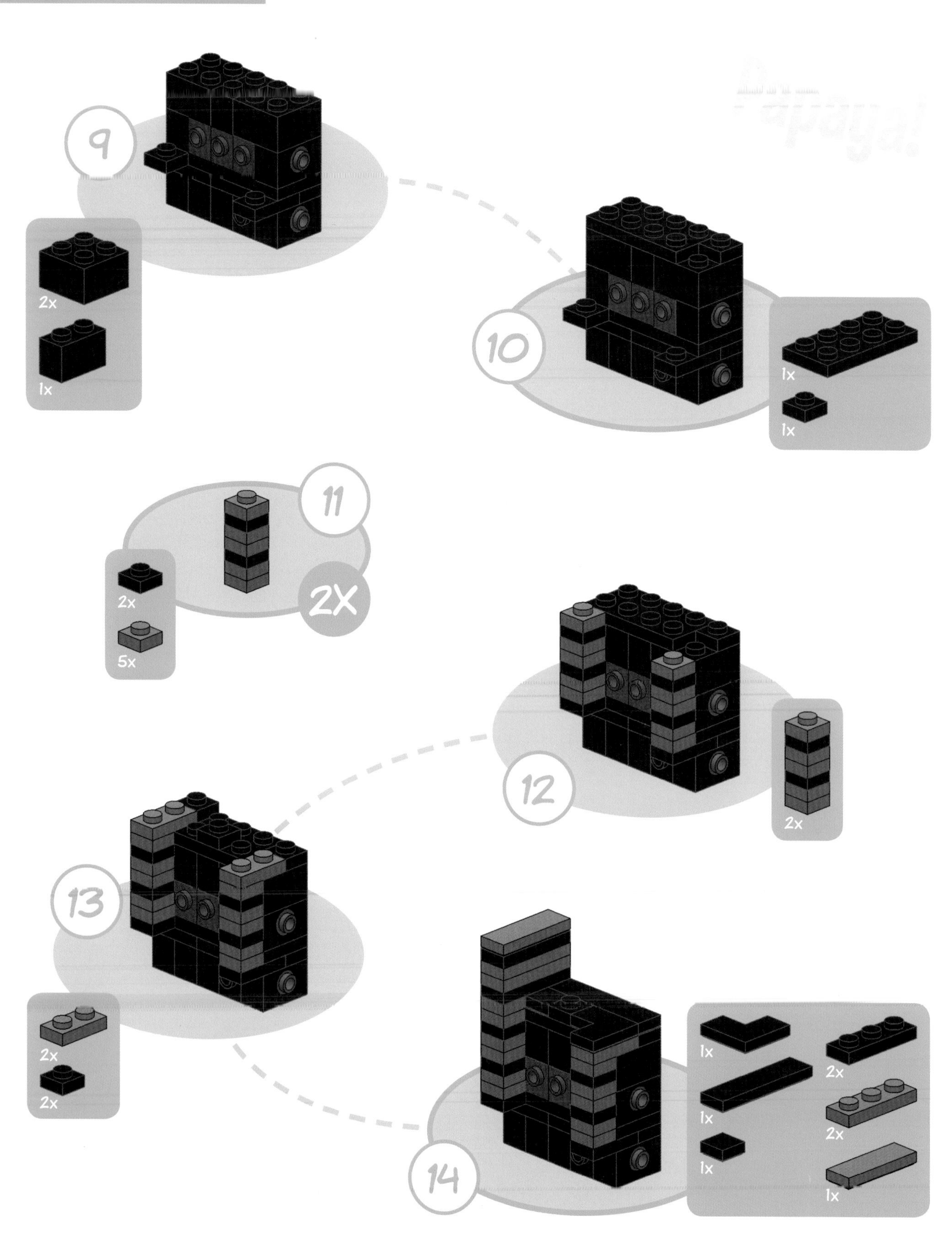
Papaya!
9
2x
1x
10
1x
1x
11
2X
2x
5x
12
2x
13
2x
2x
14
1x
2x
1x
2x
1x
1x

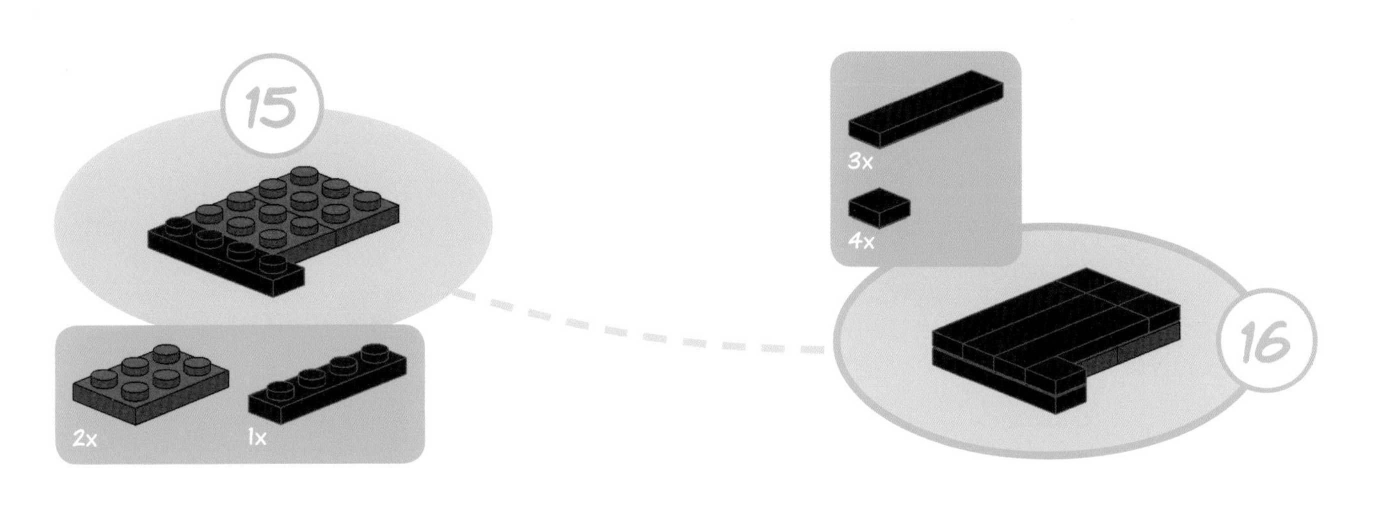
15
2x
1x
3x
4x
16

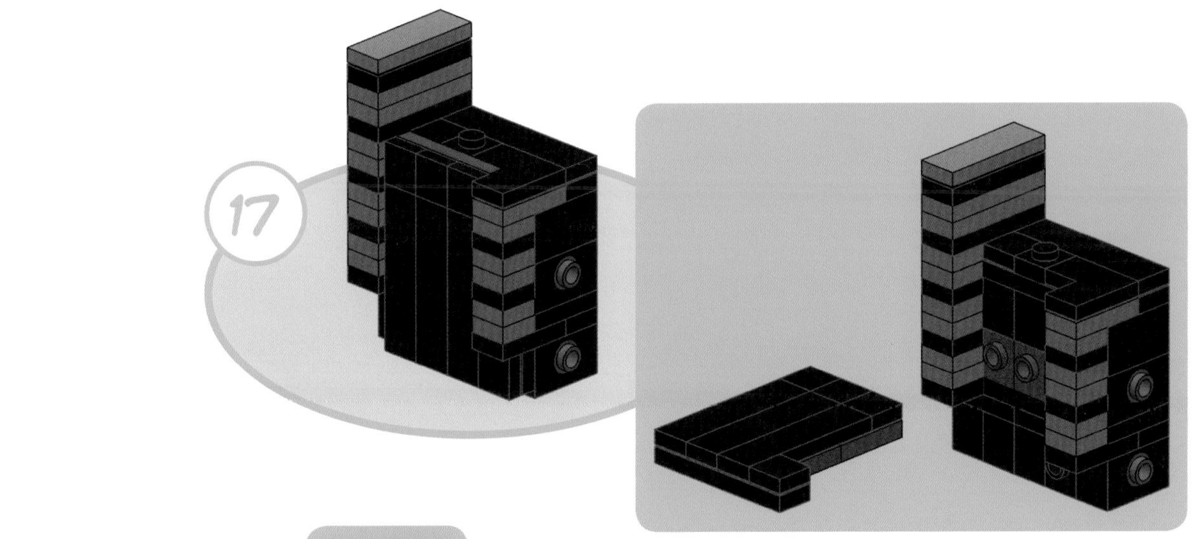
17

18

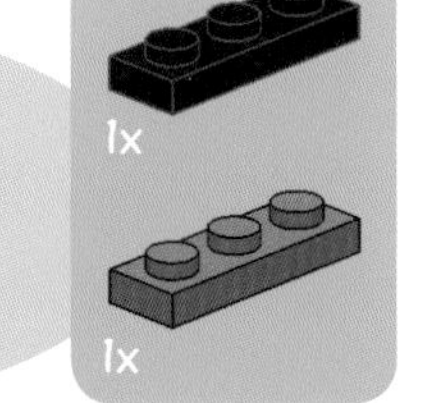
1x
1x

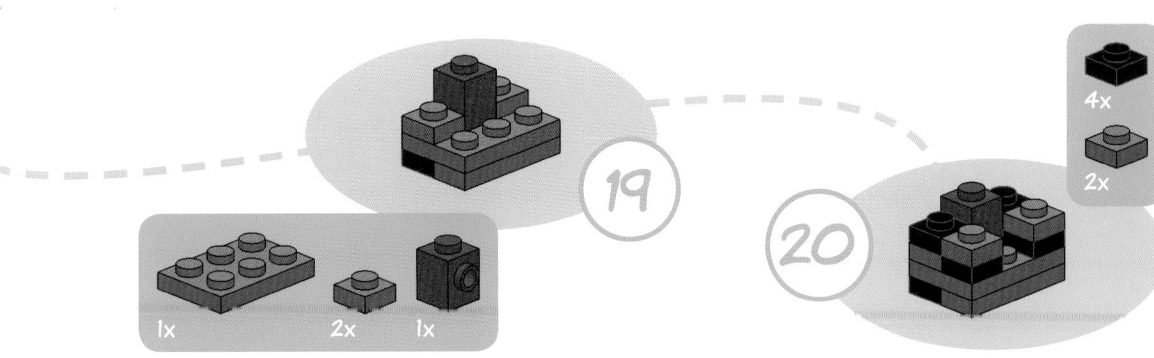
19
1x
2x
1x
4x
2x
20

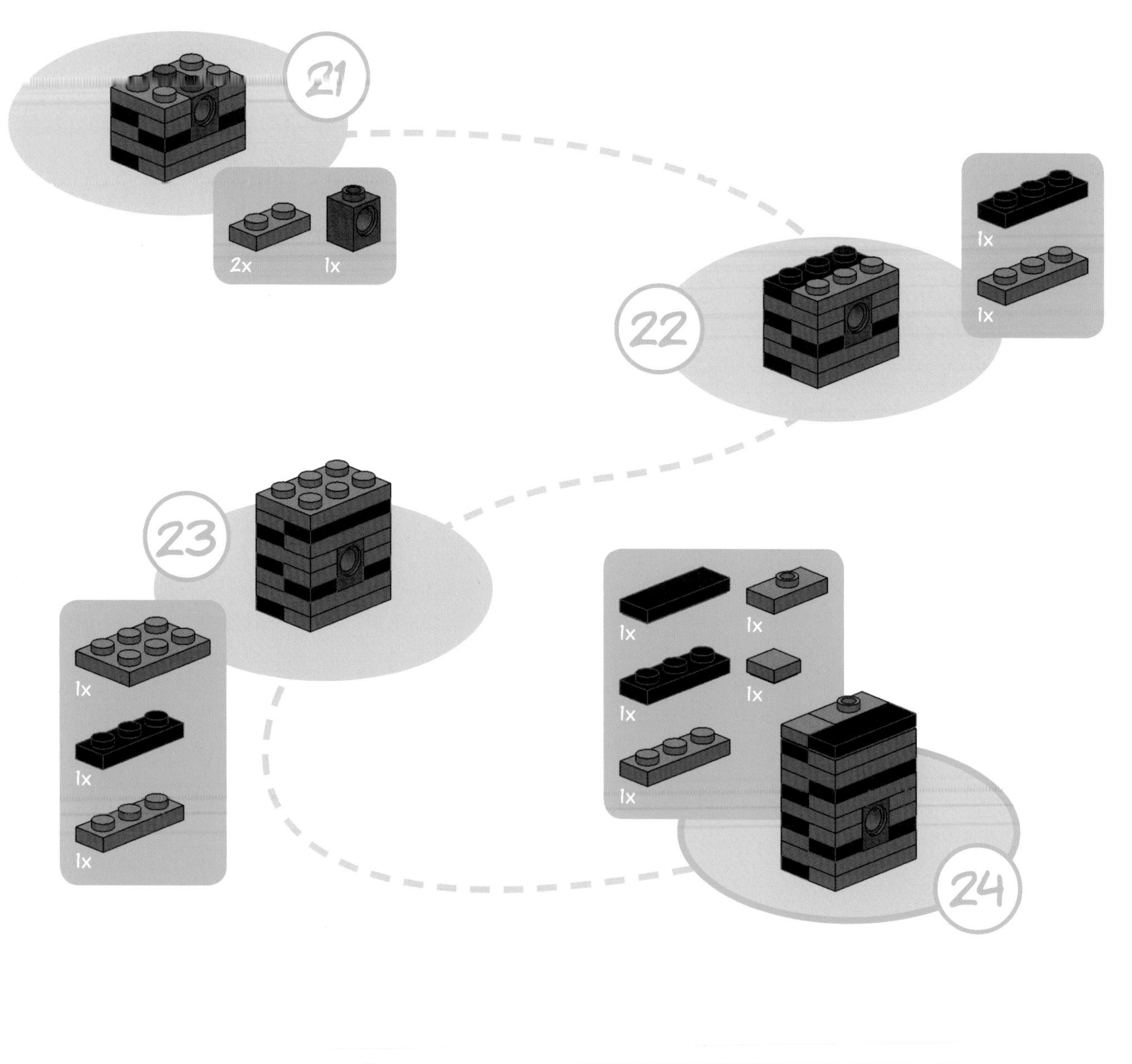
21
2x
1x
1x
1x
22
23
1x
1x
1x
1x
1x
1x
1x
1x
1x
24

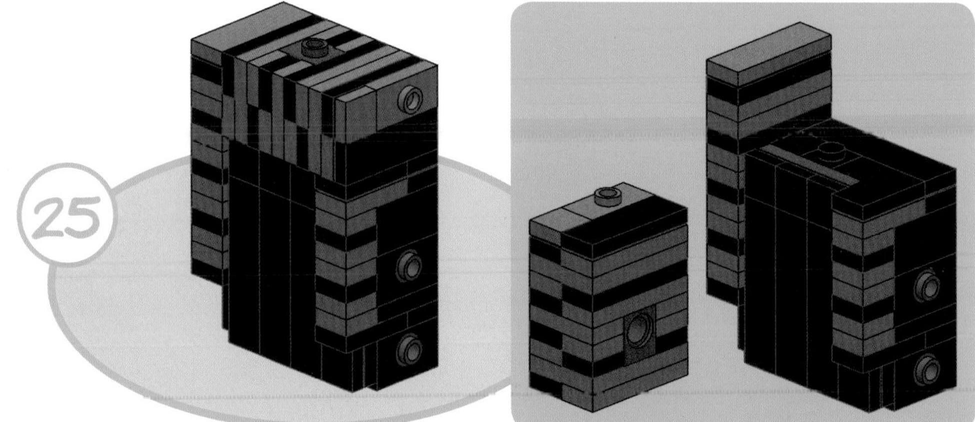
25

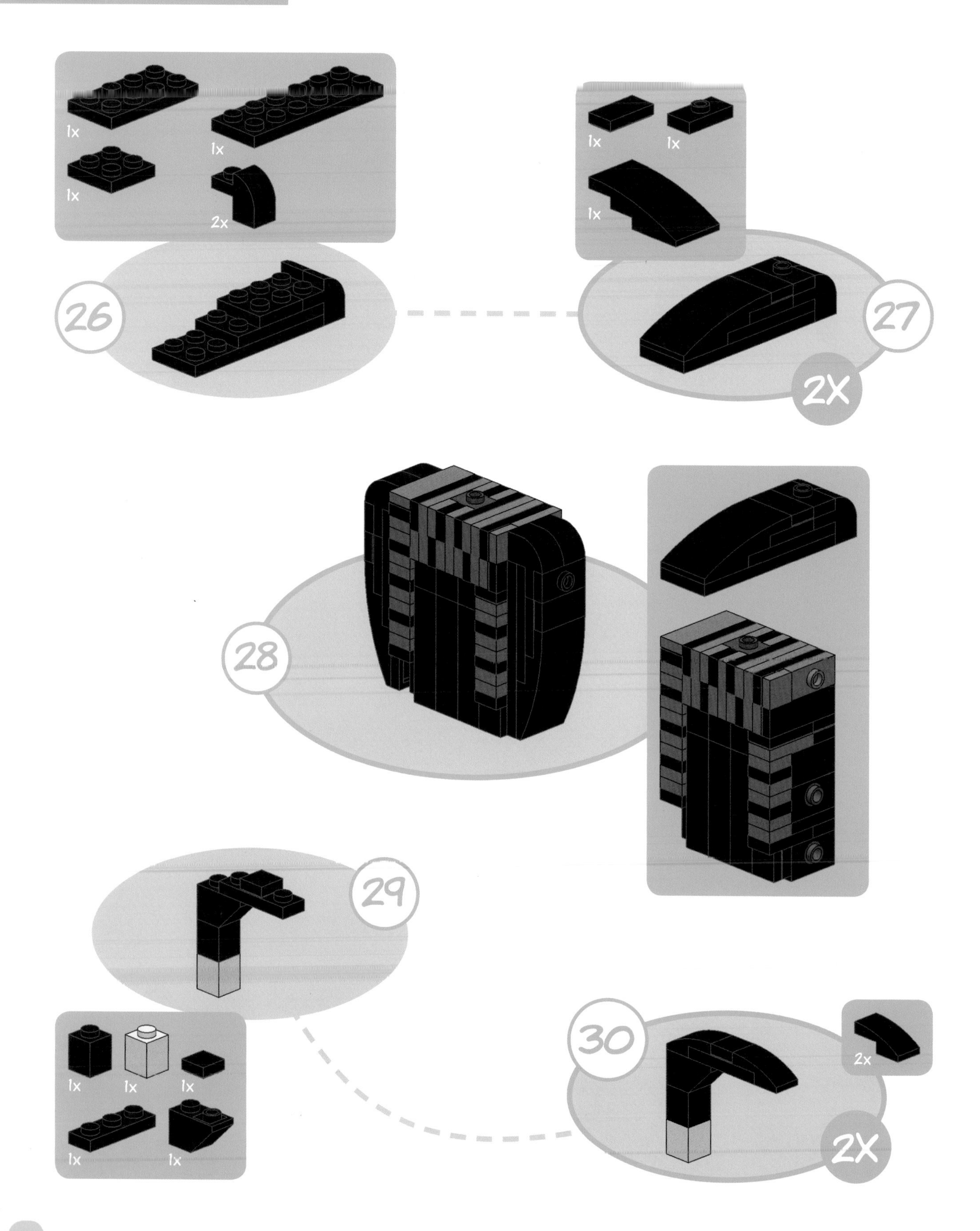
1x
1x
1x
2x
26
1x
1x
1x
27
2X
28
29
1x
1x
1x
1x
1x
30
2x
2X

31
2x
32
2X
1x
2x

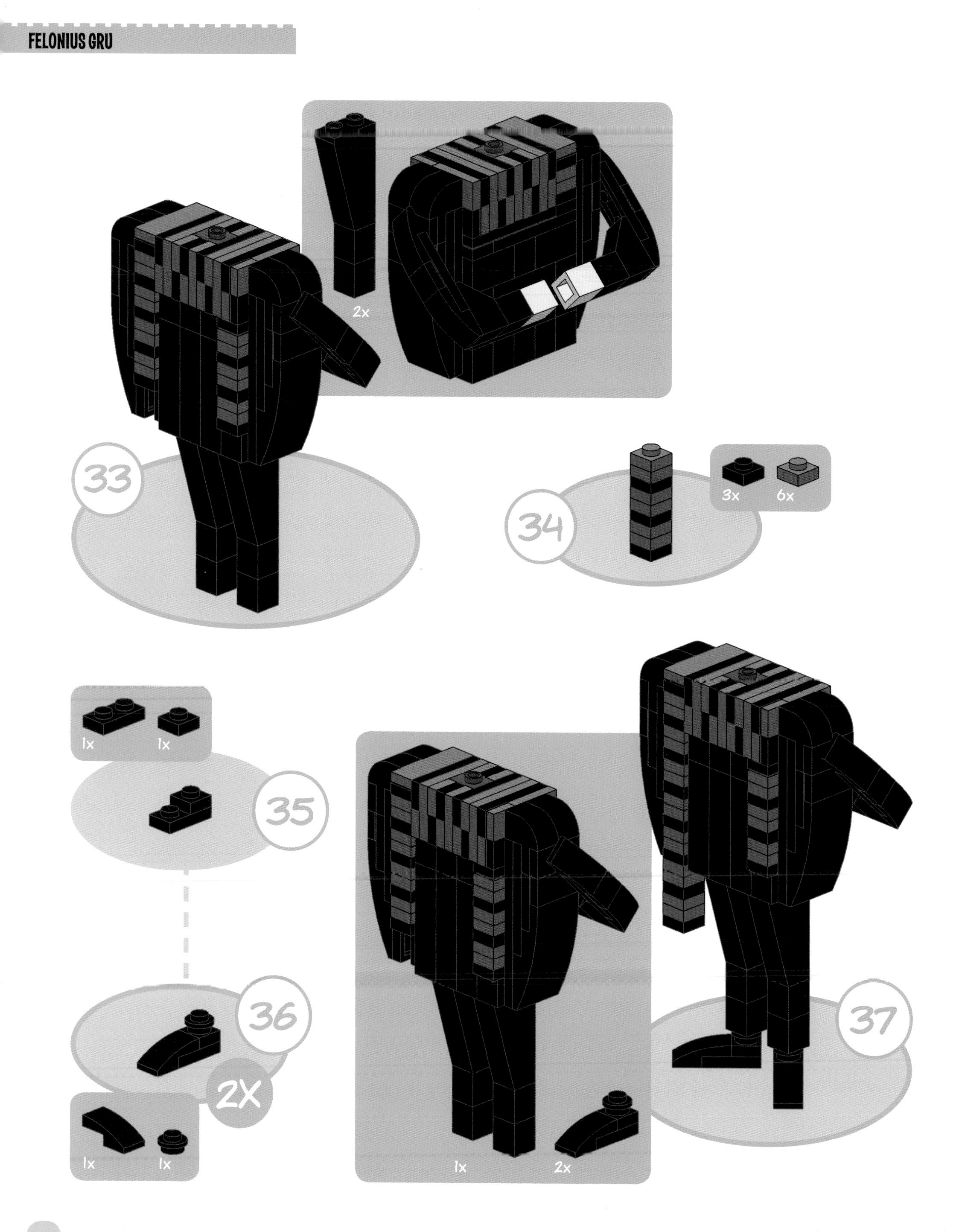
2x
33
34
3x
6x
1x
1x
35
36
2X
1x
1x
1x
2x
37

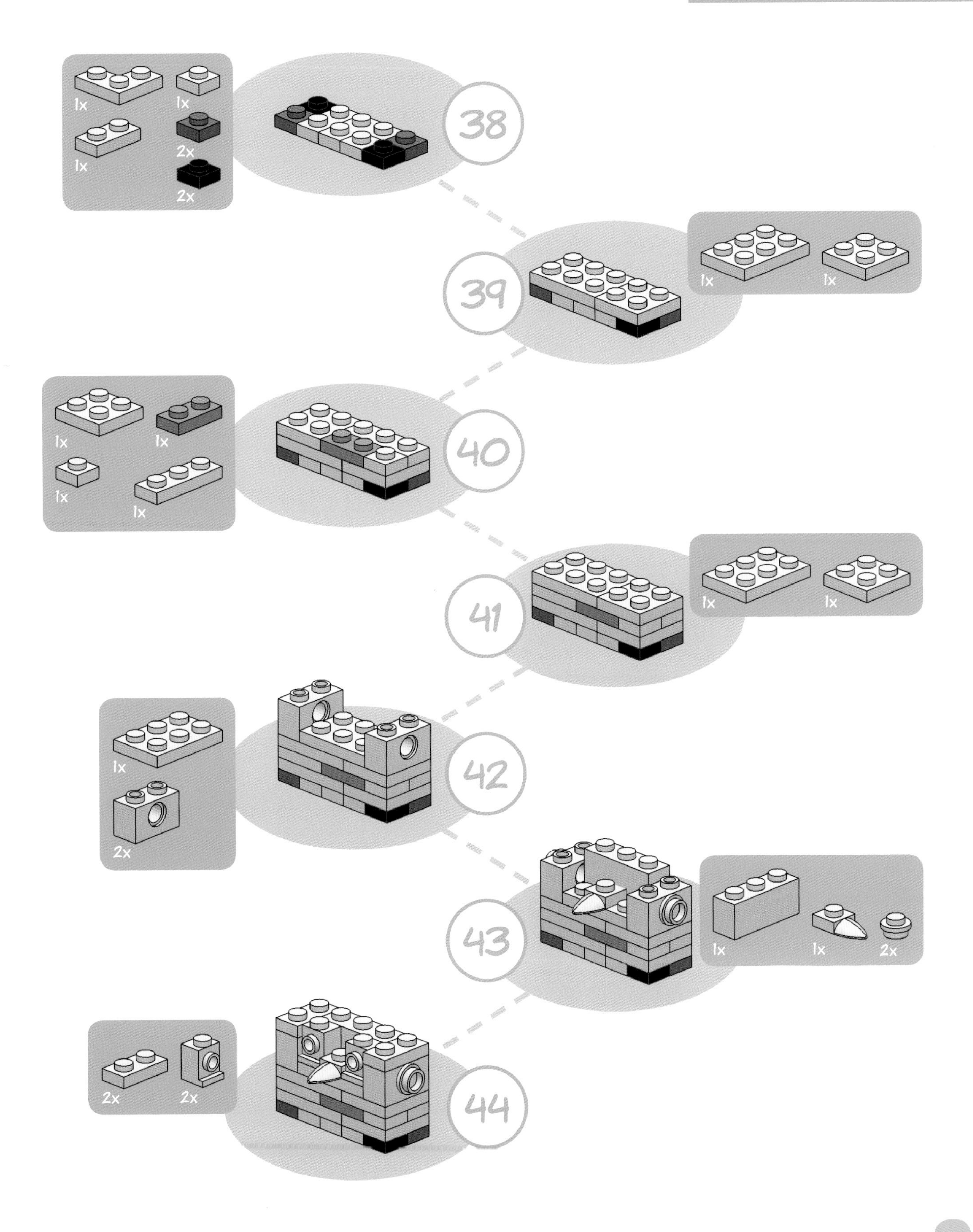
38
1x
1x
1x
2x
2x
39
1x
1x
40
1x
1x
1x
1x
41
1x
1x
42
1x
2x
43
1x
1x
2x
44
2x
2x

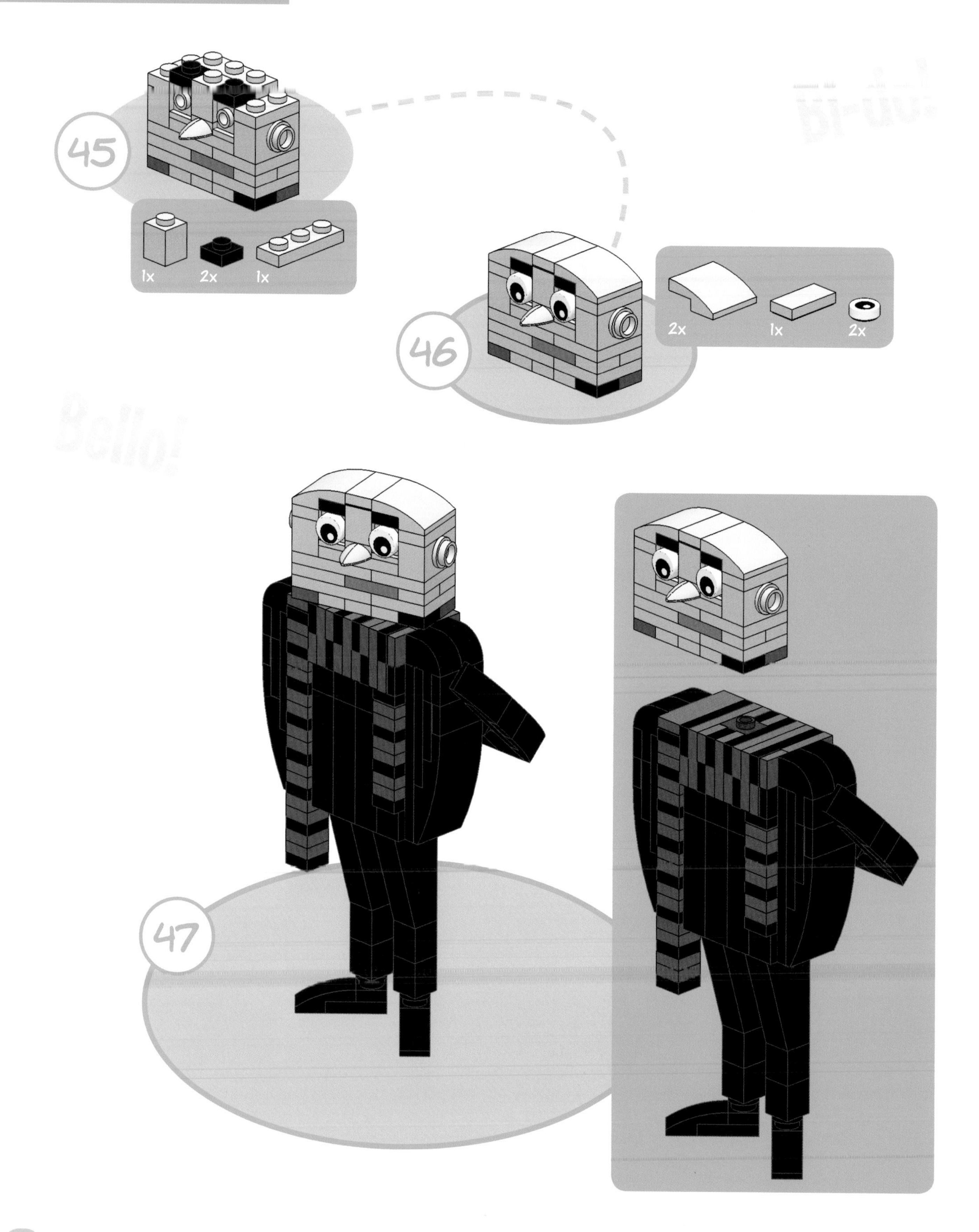
45
1x
2x
1x
46
2x
1x
2x
Bello!
47

PARTS LIST

Quantity	Color	Element	Element Name	LEGO® Number
7	Black	3005	Brick 1 x 1	300526
3	Tan	3005	Brick 1 x 1	4113915
2	Tan	4070	Brick 1 x 1 with Headlight	4118793
1	Black	87087	Brick 1 x 1 with Stud on 1 Side	4558954
4	Red	87087	Brick 1 x 1 with Stud on 1 Side	4558886
1	Black	3004	Brick 1 x 2	300426
1	Black	3622	Brick 1 x 3	362226
1	Tan	3622	Brick 1 x 3	4162465
4	Black	6091	Brick 2 x 1 x 1 & 1/3 with Curved Top	609126
2	Black	3003	Brick 2 x 2	300326
19	Black	3024	Plate 1 x 1	302426
22	Dark Bluish Gray	3024	Plate 1 x 1	4210719
2	Tan	3024	Plate 1 x 1	4159553
2	Black	4073	Plate 1 x 1 Round	614126
2	Tan	4073	Plate 1 x 1 Round	4161734
1	Tan	49668	Plate 1 x 1 with Tooth In-line	4224793
3	Black	3023	Plate 1 x 2	302326
4	Dark Bluish Gray	3023	Plate 1 x 2	4211063
1	Dark Tan	3023	Plate 1 x 2	4497082, 4528604
3	Tan	3023	Plate 1 x 2	4113917
2	Black	3794	Plate 1 x 2 without Groove with 1 Centre Stud	379426
1	Dark Bluish Gray	3794	Plate 1 x 2 without Groove with 1 Centre Stud	4211119
9	Black	3623	Plate 1 x 3	362326
6	Dark Bluish Gray	3623	Plate 1 x 3	4211133
2	Tan	3623	Plate 1 x 3	4121921
2	Black	3710	Plate 1 x 4	371026
2	Black	3022	Plate 2 x 2	302226
3	Tan	3022	Plate 2 x 2	4114084
1	Black	2420	Plate 2 x 2 Corner	242026
1	Tan	2420	Plate 2 x 2 Corner	4114077
2	Dark Bluish Gray	3021	Plate 2 x 3	4211043
2	Red	3021	Plate 2 x 3	302121
3	Tan	3021	Plate 2 x 3	30215, 4118790
4	Black	3020	Plate 2 x 4	302026
2	Black	3795	Plate 2 x 6	379526

Quantity	Color	Element	Element Name	LEGO® Number
2	Black	3665	Slope Brick 45 2 x 1 Inverted without Inner Stopper Ring	366526
2	Black	2449	Slope Brick 75 2 x 1 x 3 Inverted	244926, 4636202
6	Black	11477	Slope Brick Curved 2 x 1	6047276
2	Tan	15068	Slope Brick Curved 2 x 2 x 0.667	6046924
2	Black	93606	Slope Brick Curved 4 x 2	4647286
1	Dark Tan	6587	Technic Axle 3 with Stud	4566927, 6031821
1	Red	6541	Technic Brick 1 x 1 with Hole	654121
2	Black	32064b	Technic Brick 1 x 2 with Axlehole Type 2	4233487
4	Black	3700	Technic Brick 1 x 2 with Hole	370026
2	Tan	3700	Technic Brick 1 x 2 with Hole	4205107
3	Blue	4274	Technic Pin 1/2	4143005
2	White	98138p07	Tile 1 x 1 Round with Eye Pattern	unbekannt
7	Black	3070b	Tile 1 x 1 with Groove	307026
1	Dark Bluish Gray	3070b	Tile 1 x 1 with Groove	4210848
2	Black	3069b	Tile 1 x 2 with Groove	306926
1	Tan	3069b	Tile 1 x 2 with Groove	30695, 4114026
1	Black	63864	Tile 1 x 3 with Groove	4558170
1	Dark Bluish Gray	63864	Tile 1 x 3 with Groove	4568734
4	Black	2431	Tile 1 x 4 with Groove	243126
1	Black	14719	Tile 2 x 2 Corner	6133722

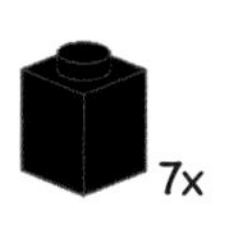

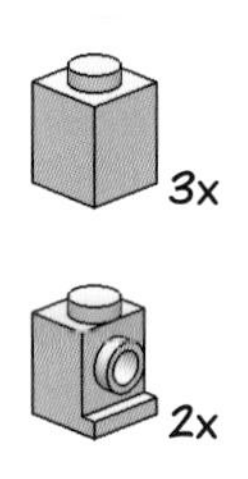

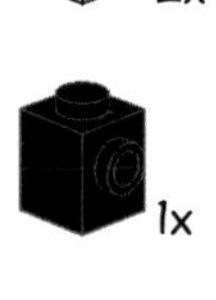

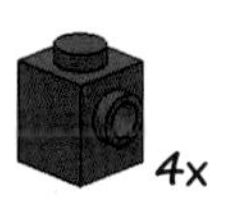

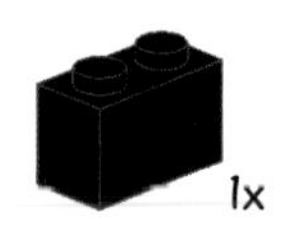

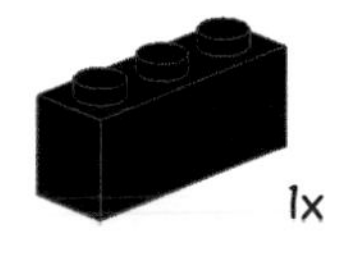

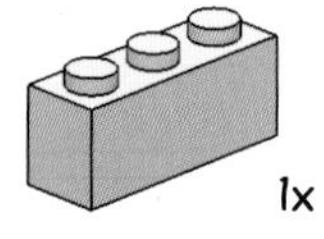

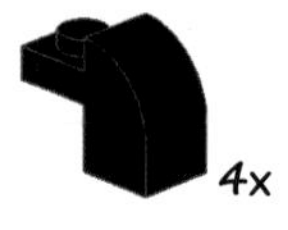

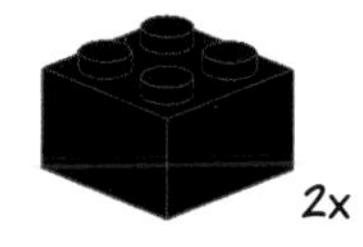

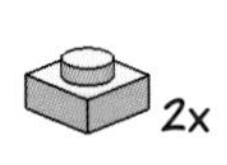

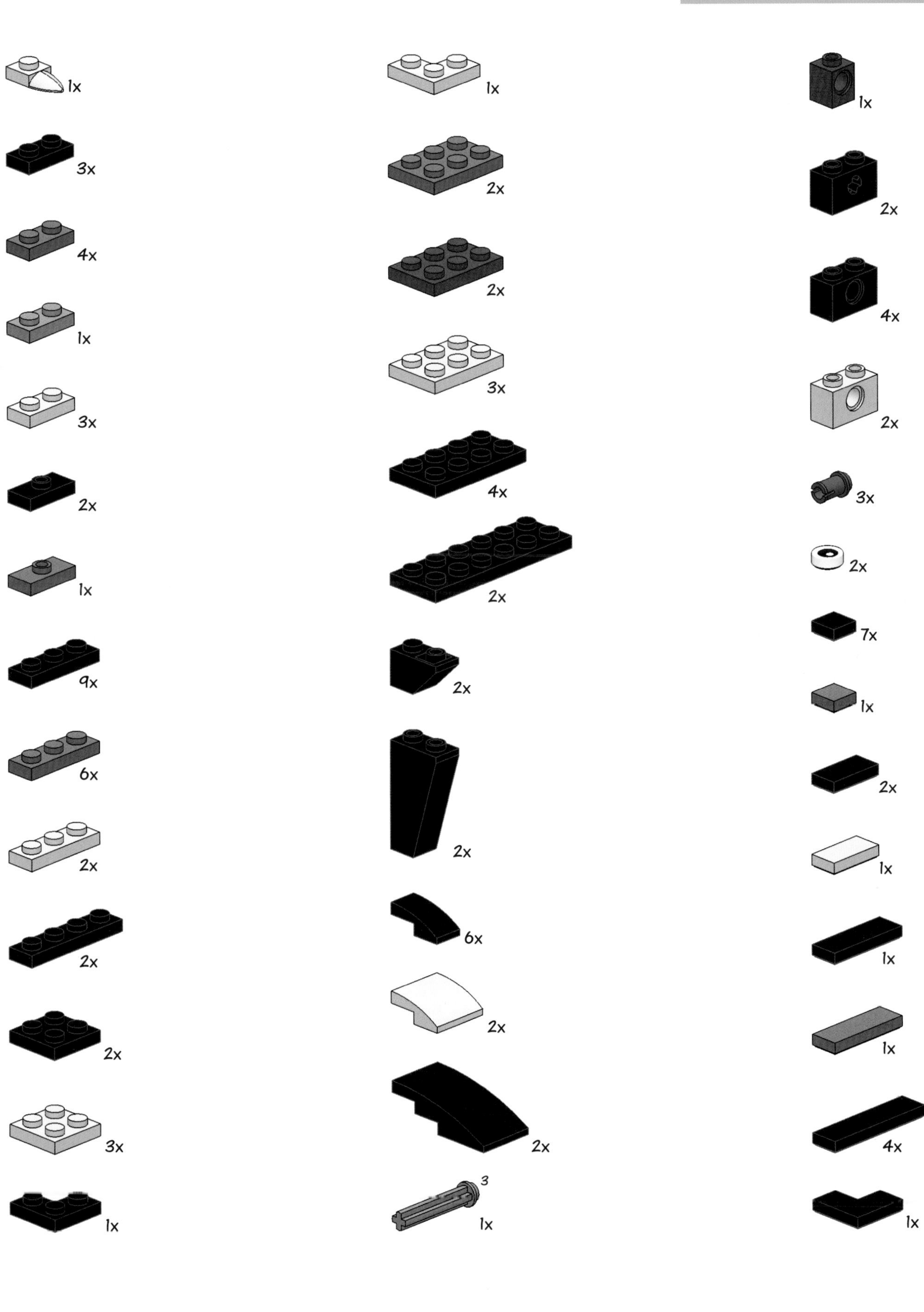
1x
3x
4x
1x
3x
2x
1x
9x
6x
2x
2x
2x
3x
1x
1x
2x
2x
3x
4x
2x
2x
2x
6x
2x
2x
3
1x
1x
2x
4x
2x
3x
2x
7x
1x
2x
1x
1x
1x
4x
1x

GRUMOBILE

Strange vehicles are normal for Gru. His car, the so-called Grumobile, was a special challenge. It's almost round and slanting everywhere. The engine is also quite fiddly. Despite my aspiration to use as few parts as possible for the models in this book, I didn't leave out this vehicle. As you can see from the instructions, despite everything, it still has a very simple construction. The recognition value is very high and the vehicle appears in all the films with Gru. That's why I decided to include this model.

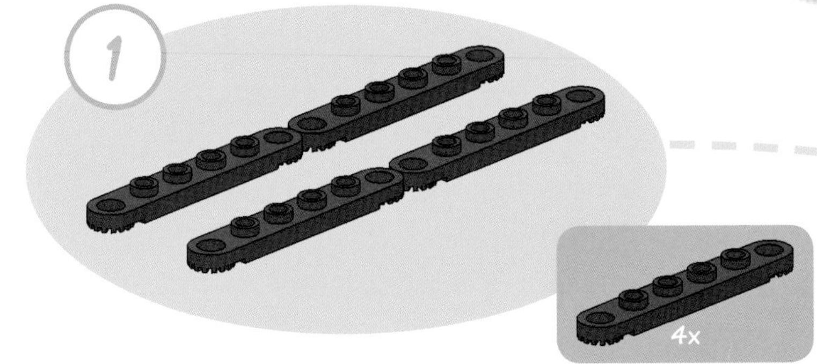

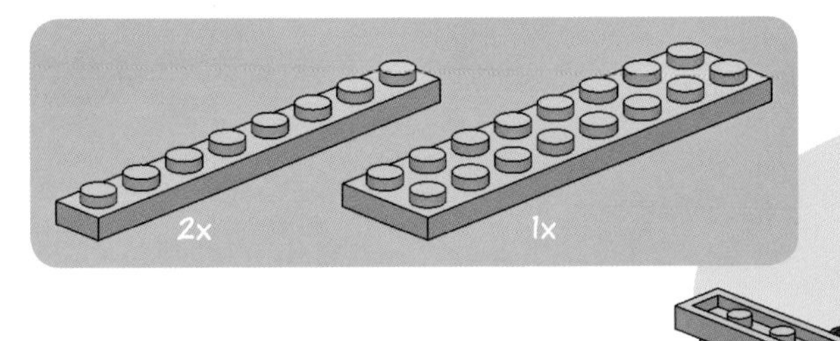

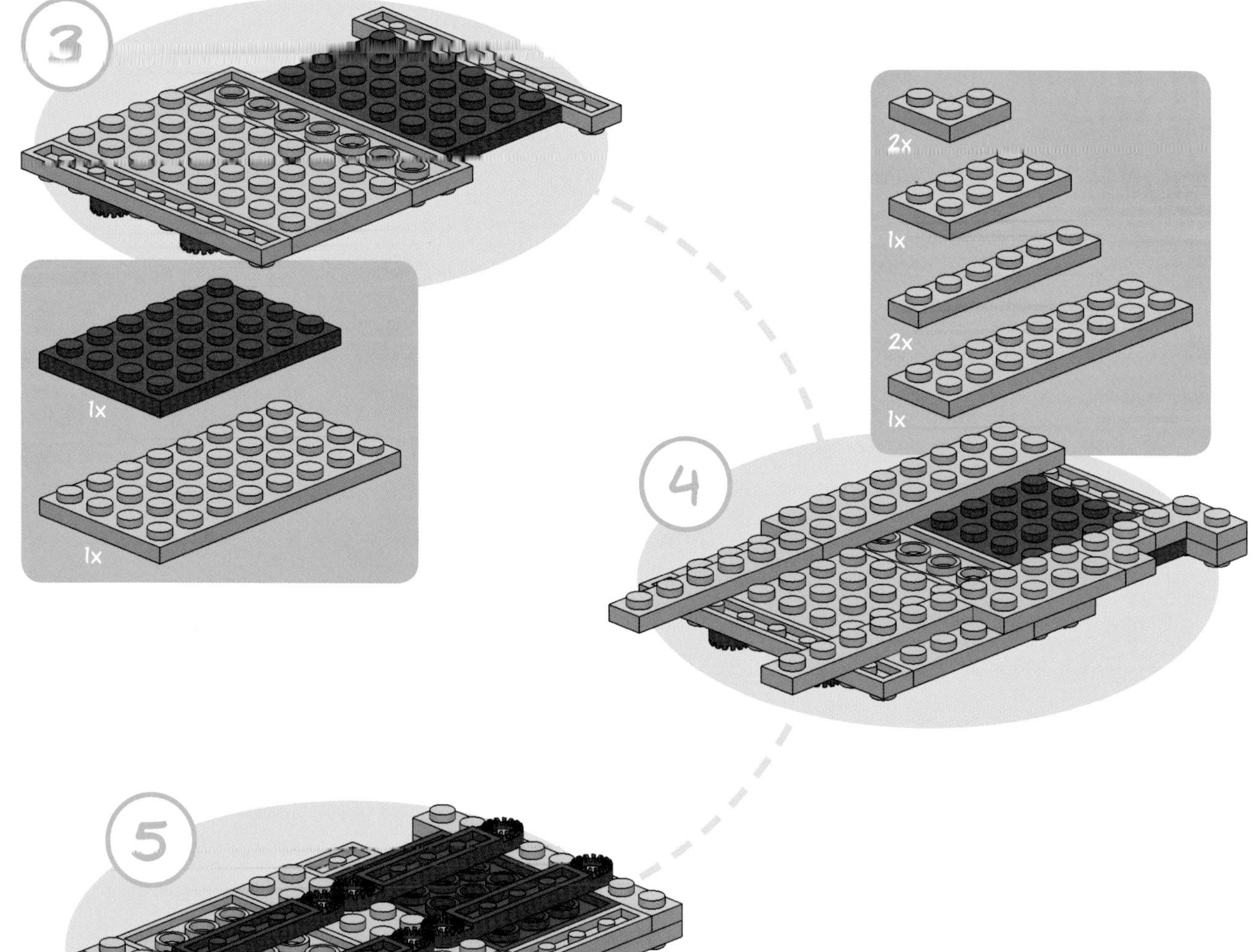

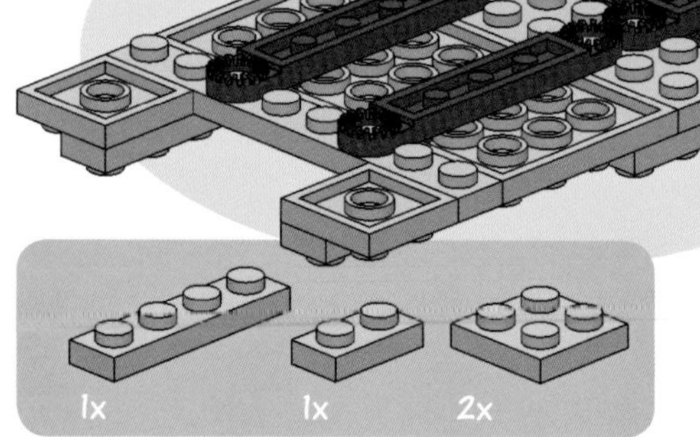

1x 1x 2x

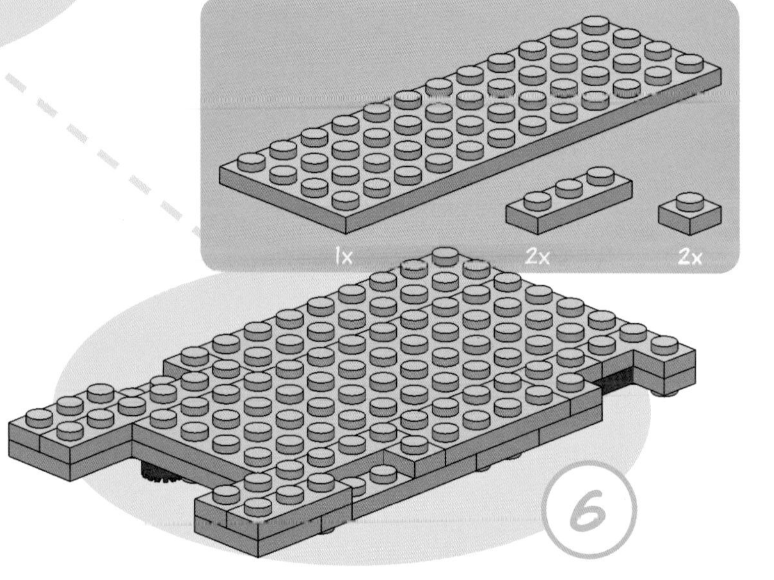

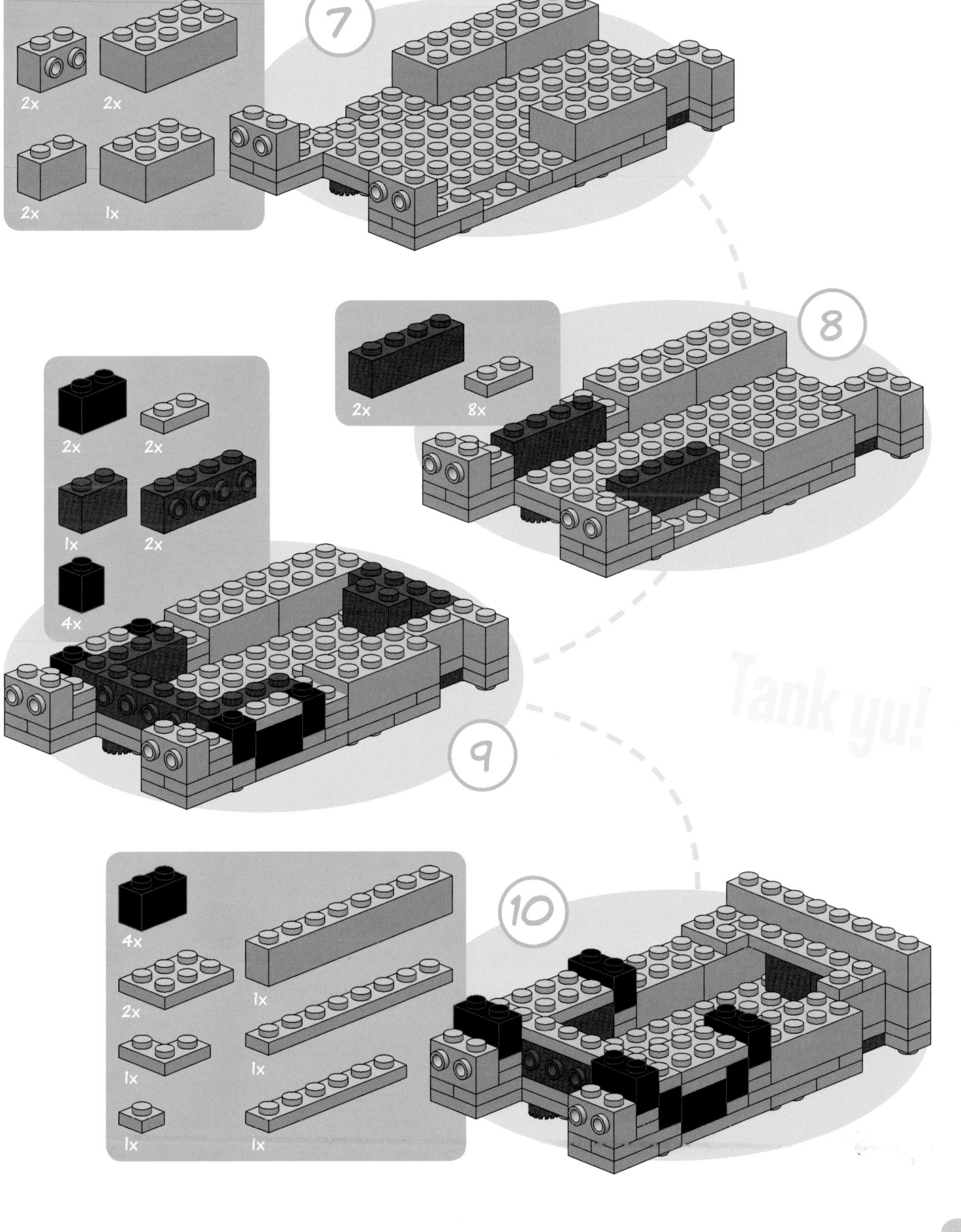
7
2x
2x
2x
1x
8
2x
8x
2x
2x
1x
2x
4x
9
Tank yu!
10
4x
1x
2x
1x
1x
1x
1x

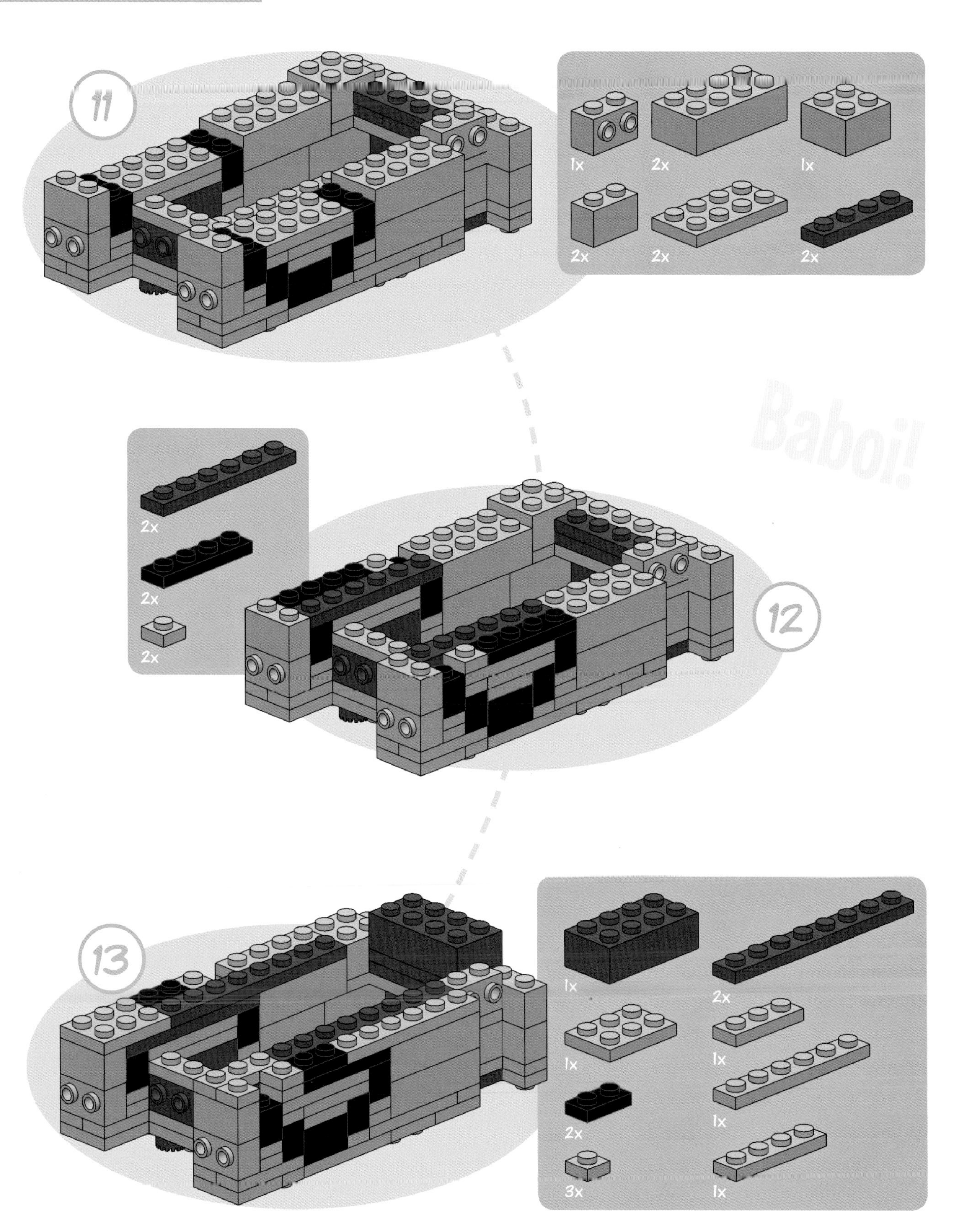
11
1x
2x
1x
2x
2x
2x
2x
2x
2x
12
13
1x
2x
1x
1x
2x
1x
3x
1x
Baboi!

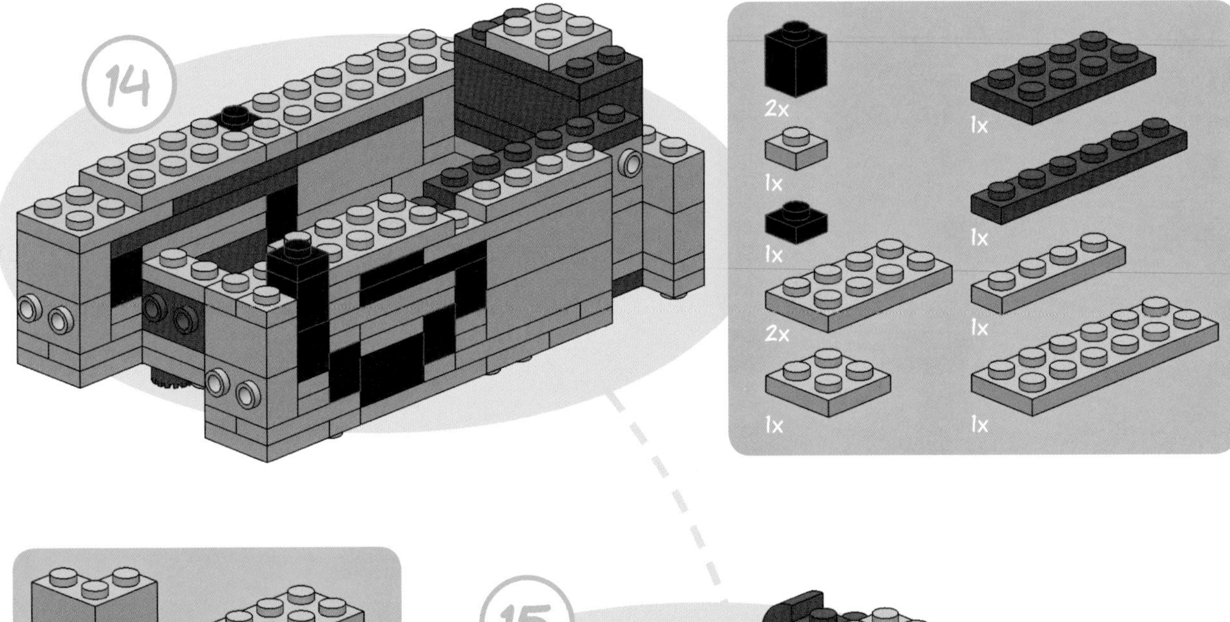
14
2x
1x
1x
2x
1x
1x
1x
1x
1x

1x
2x
2x
1x
1x
2x
15

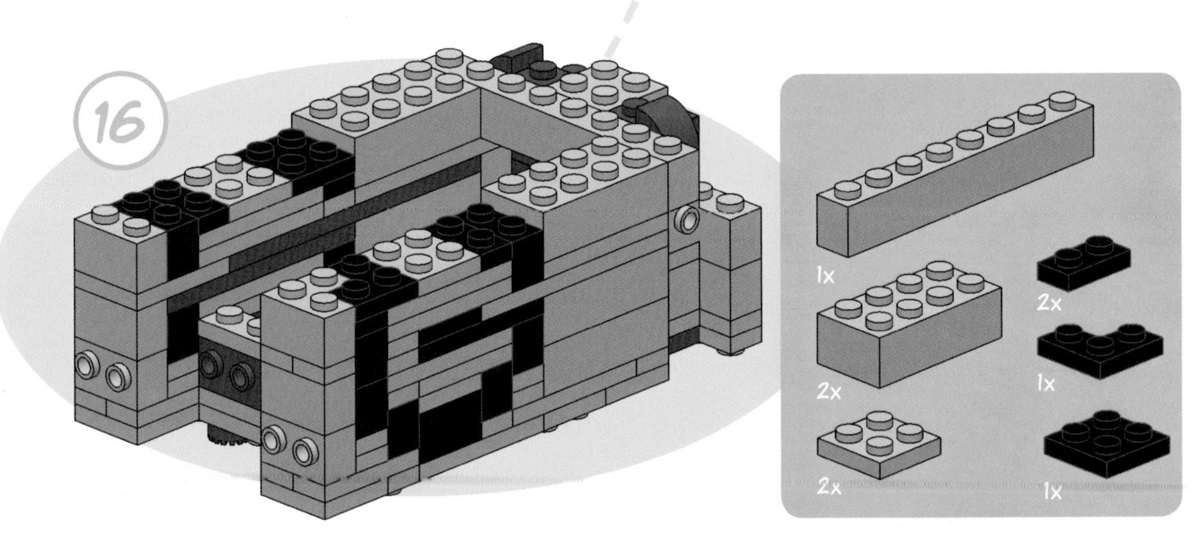
16
1x
2x
2x
2x
1x
1x

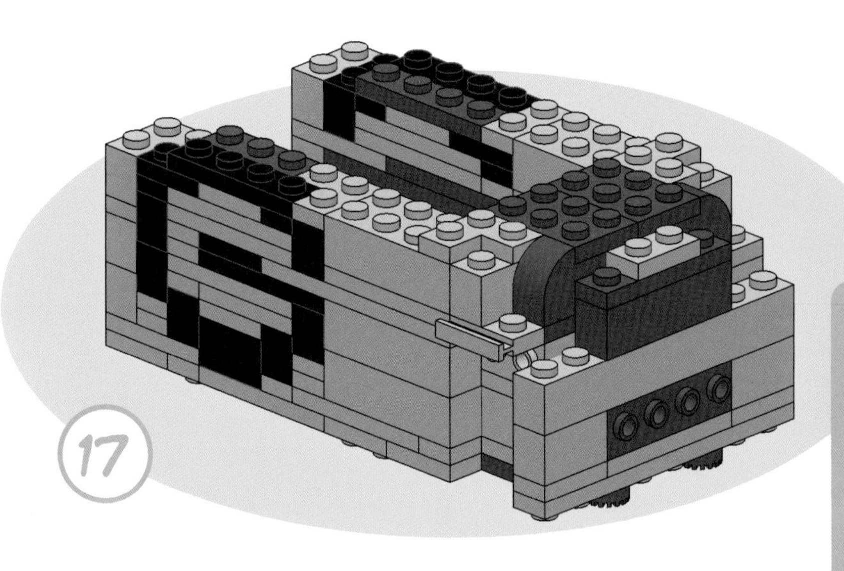

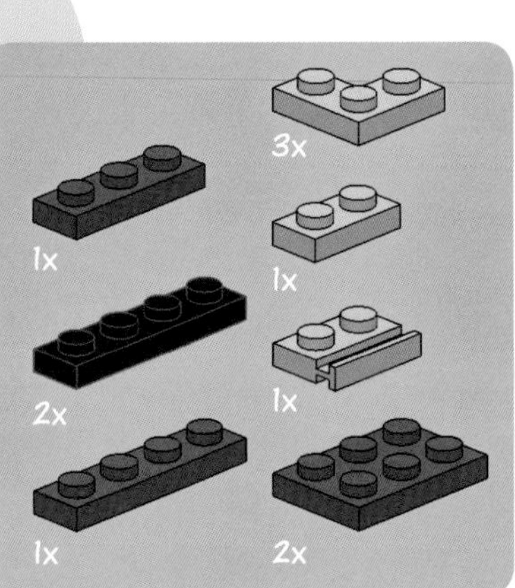

MAILBOX

These mailboxes appeared in a pre-released trailer to "Despicable Me 3." I thought they were so cute, I wanted to show you how to build them. The legs are a little tricky: I used bucket handles fixed to 2x2 plates, but not all 2x2 plates are equally suitable. If the handles don't fit the plates well, don't despair—just try another plate.

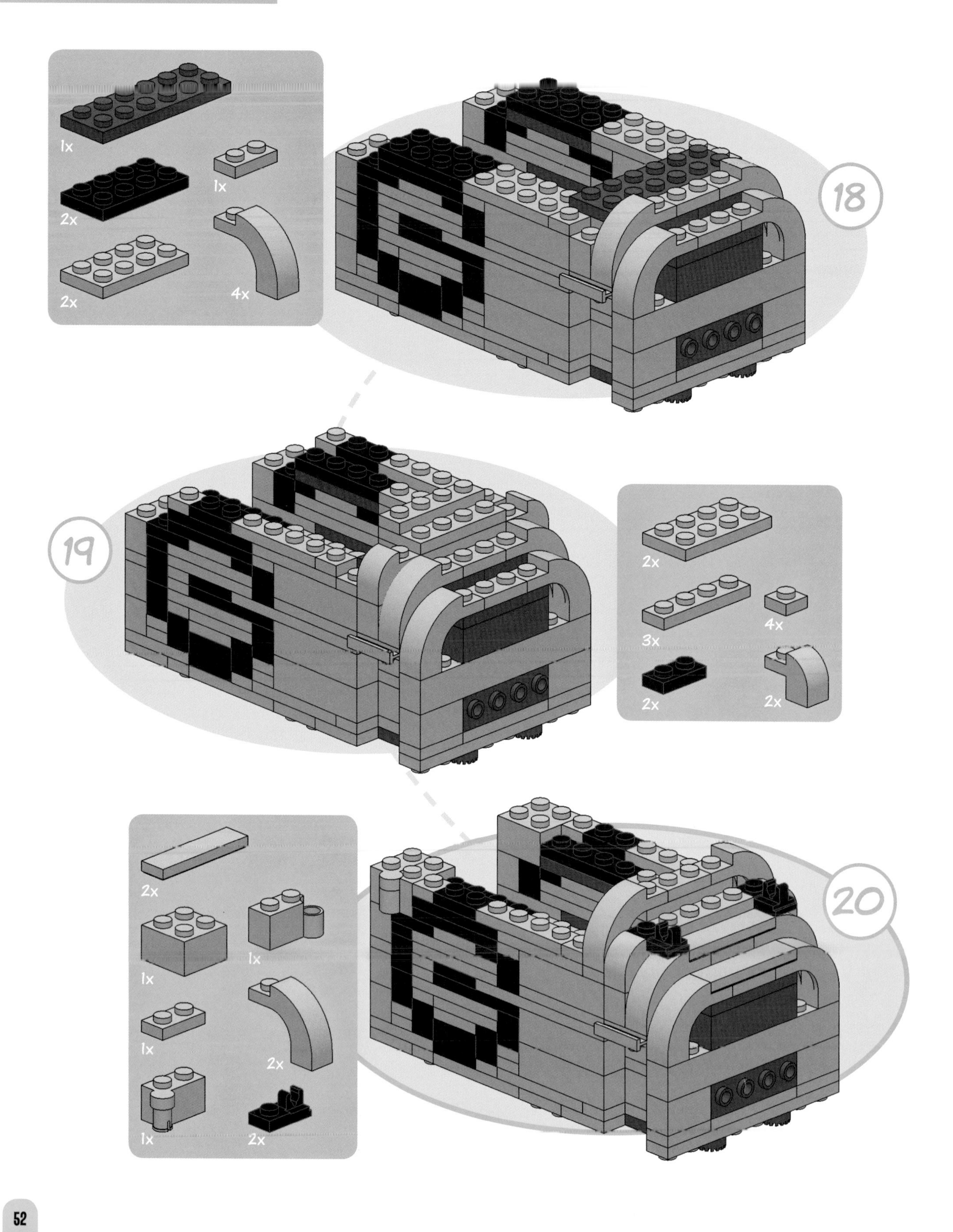
1x
1x
2x
4x
2x
18
19
2x
3x
4x
2x
2x
2x
1x
1x
1x
2x
1x
2x
20

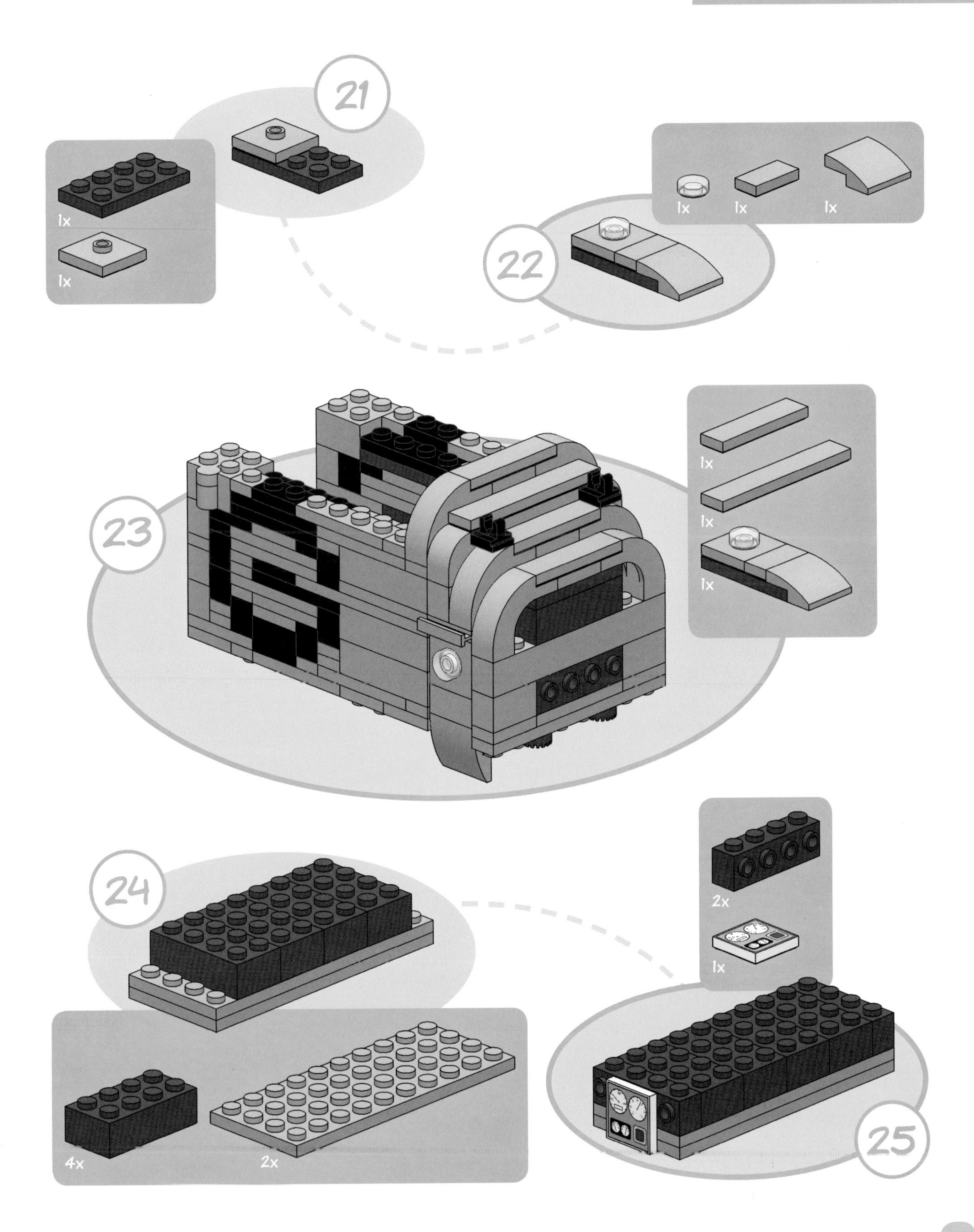
21
1x
1x
22
1x
1x
1x
23
1x
1x
1x
24
4x
2x
2x
1x
25

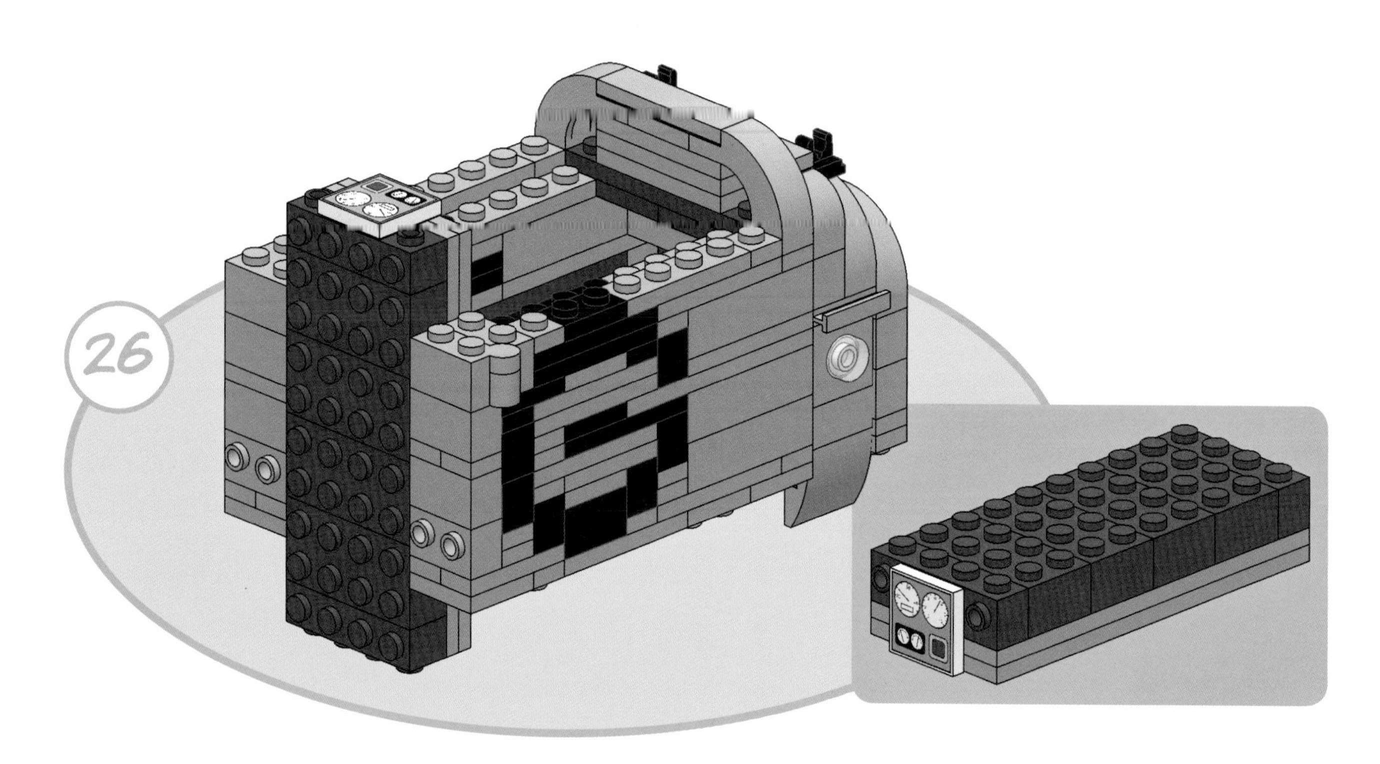
26

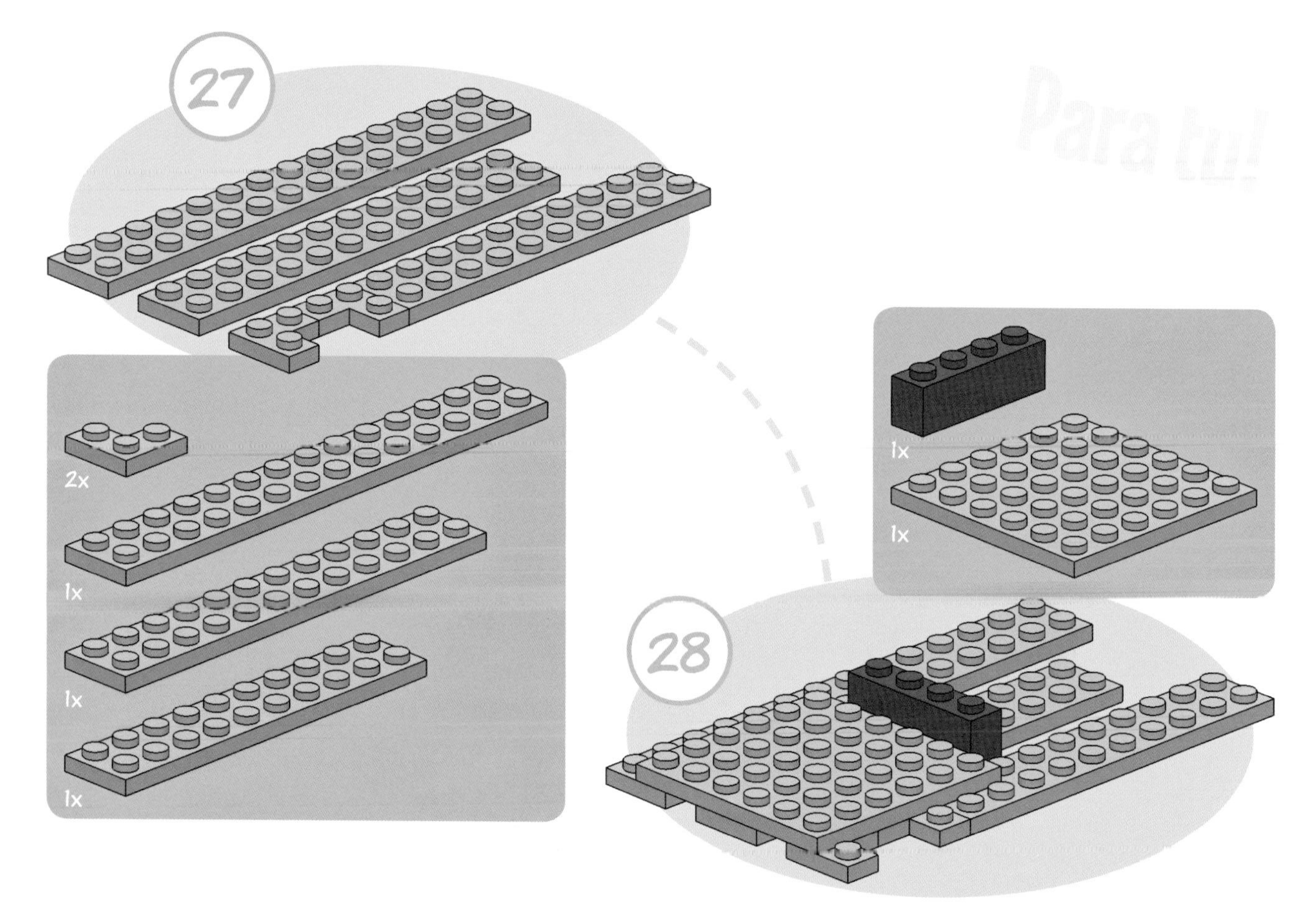
27
2x
1x
1x
1x
1x
1x
28

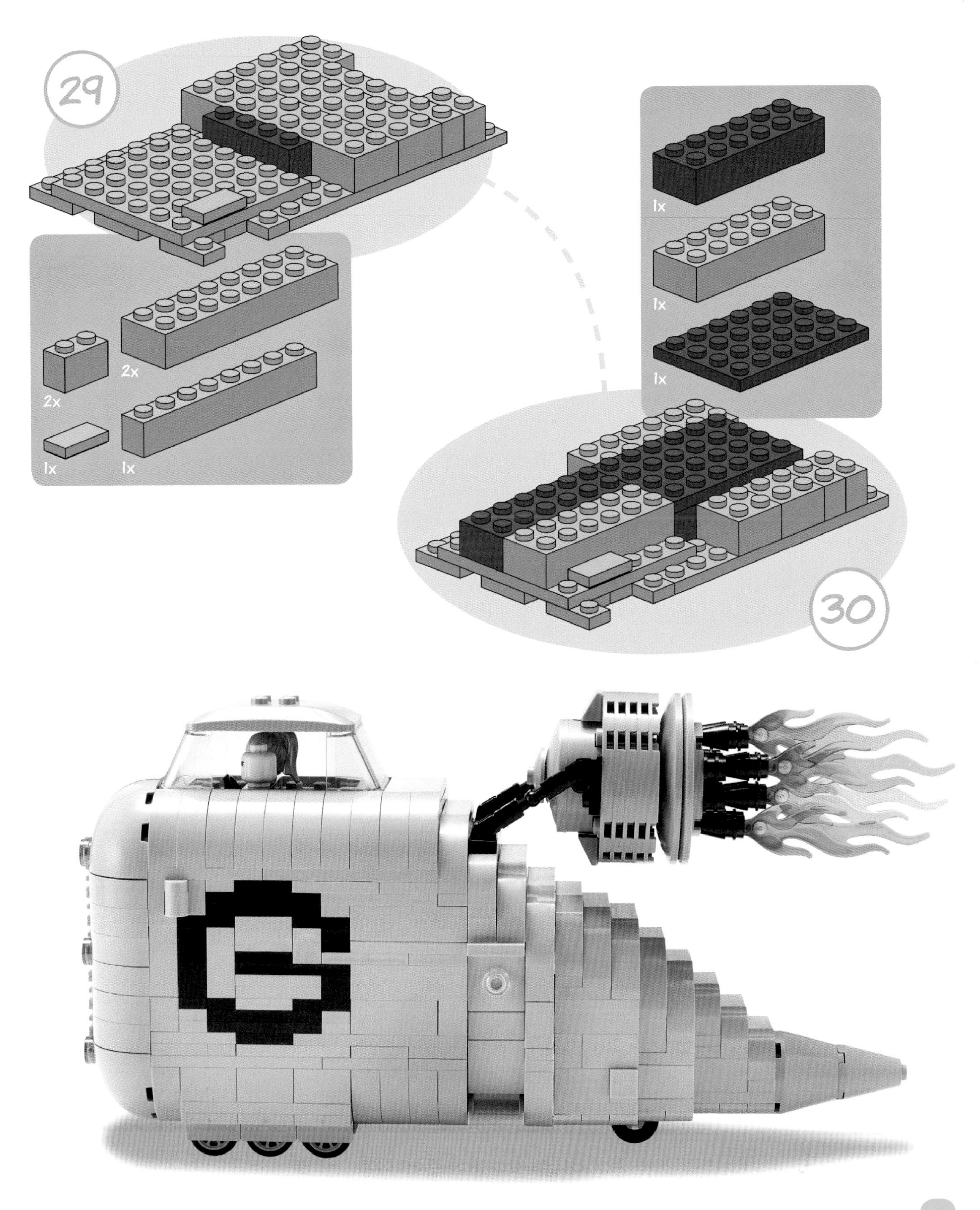

29
2x
2x
1x
1x
1x
1x
1x
30

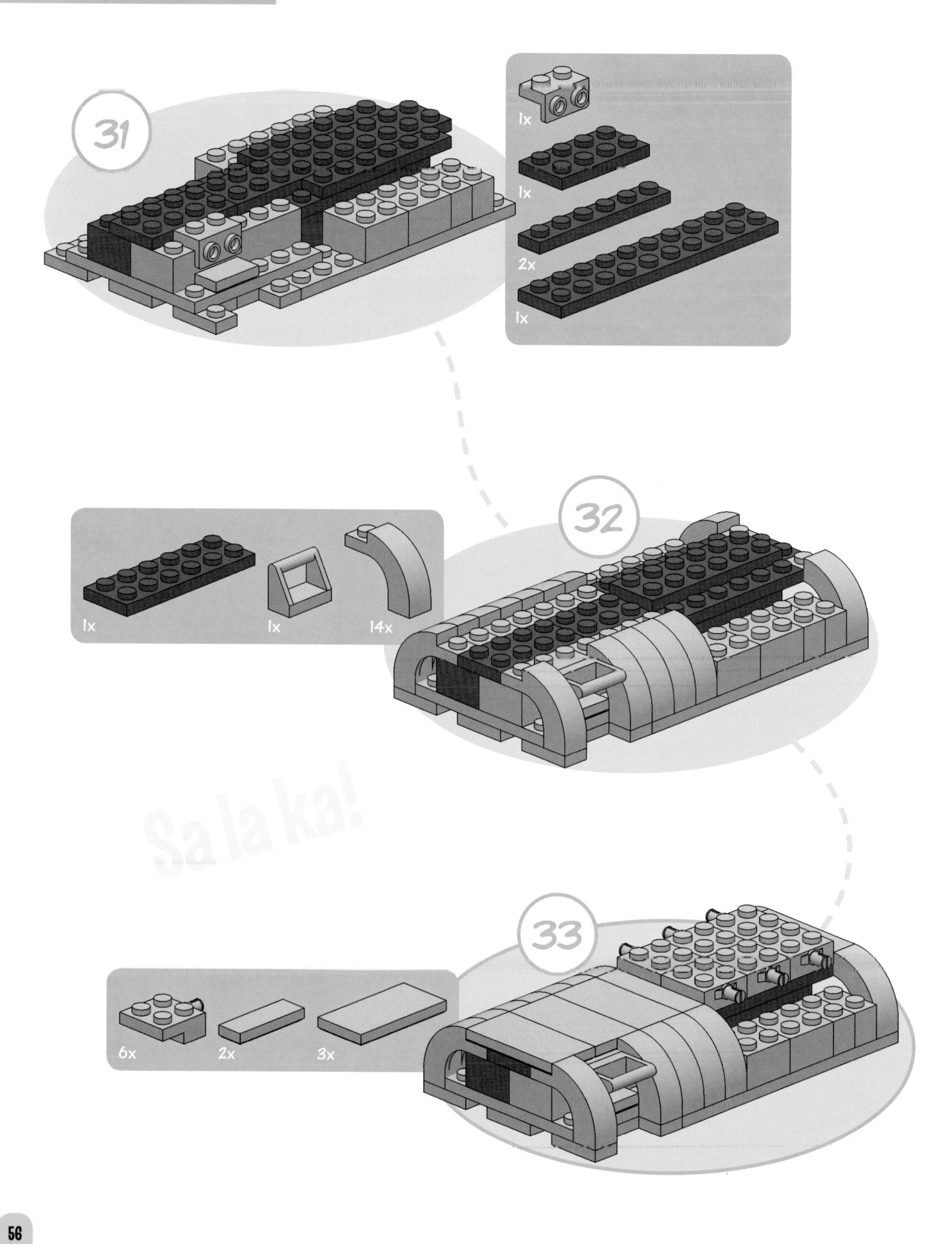
31
1x
1x
2x
1x
32
1x
1x
14x
33
6x
2x
3x
Sa la ka!

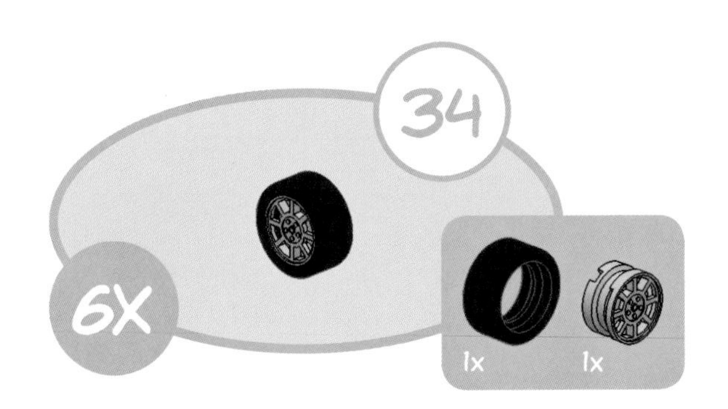
34
6X
1x
1x

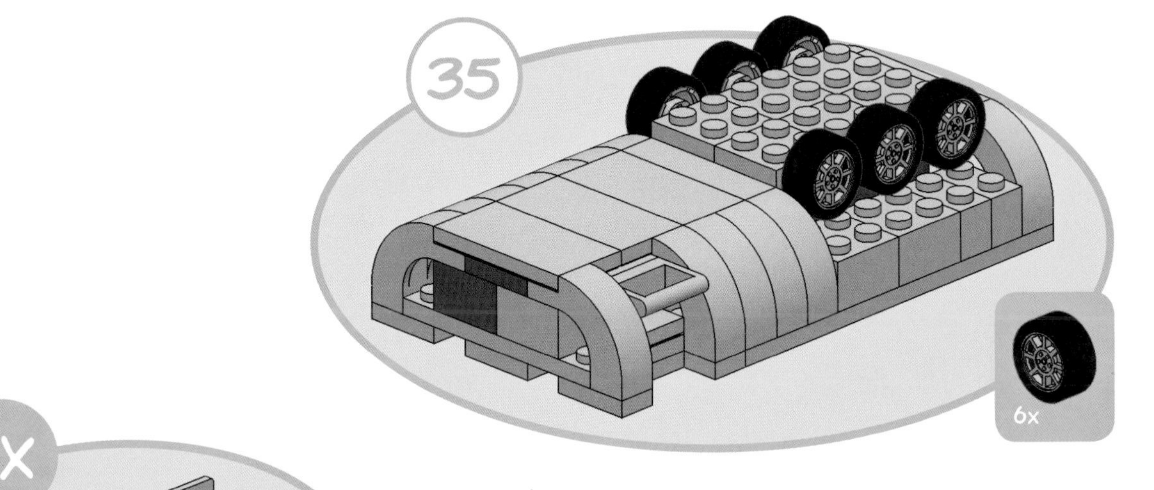
35
6x

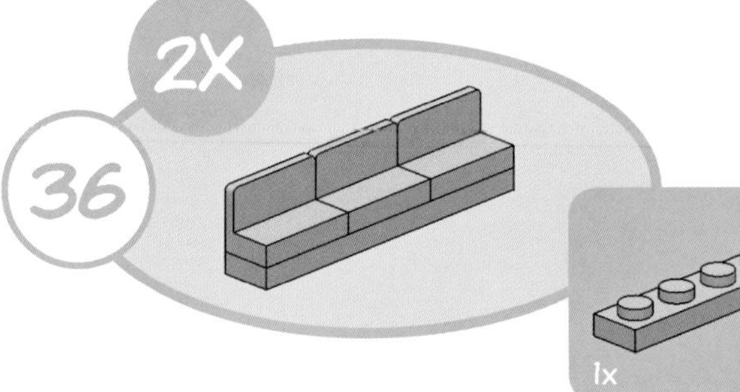
2X
36
1x
3x

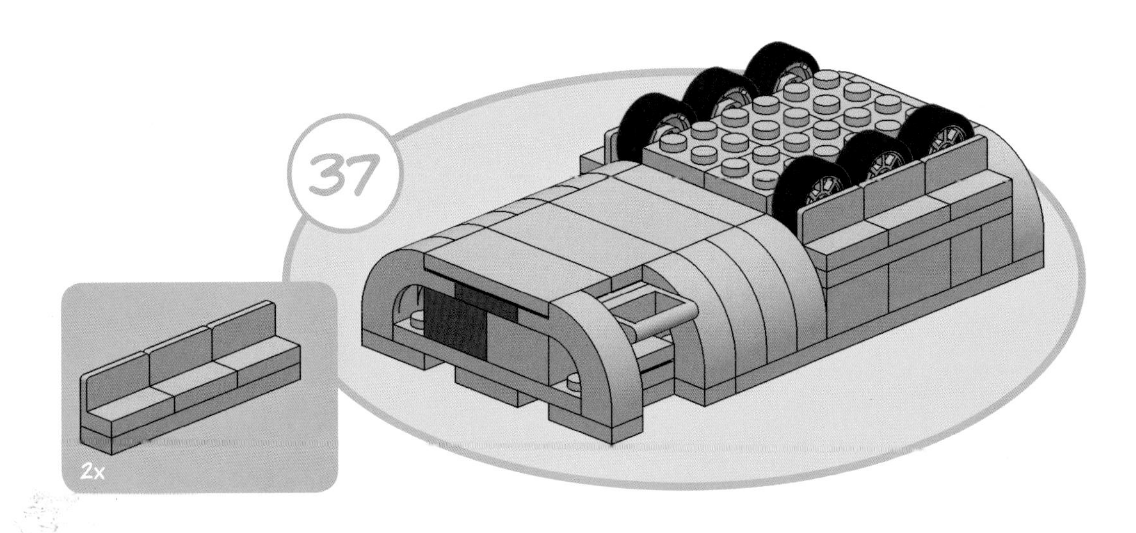
37
2x

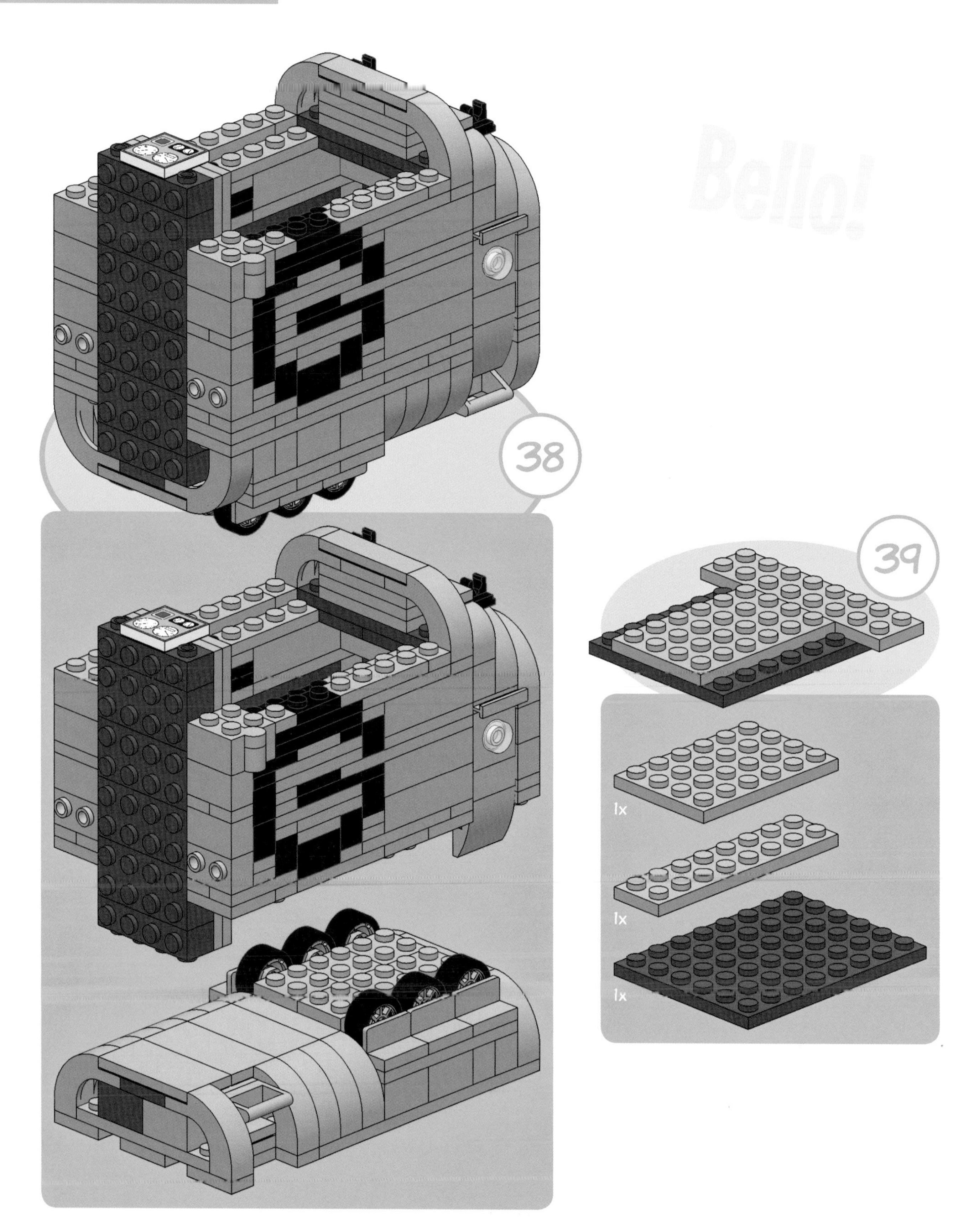
Bello!
38
39
1x
1x
1x

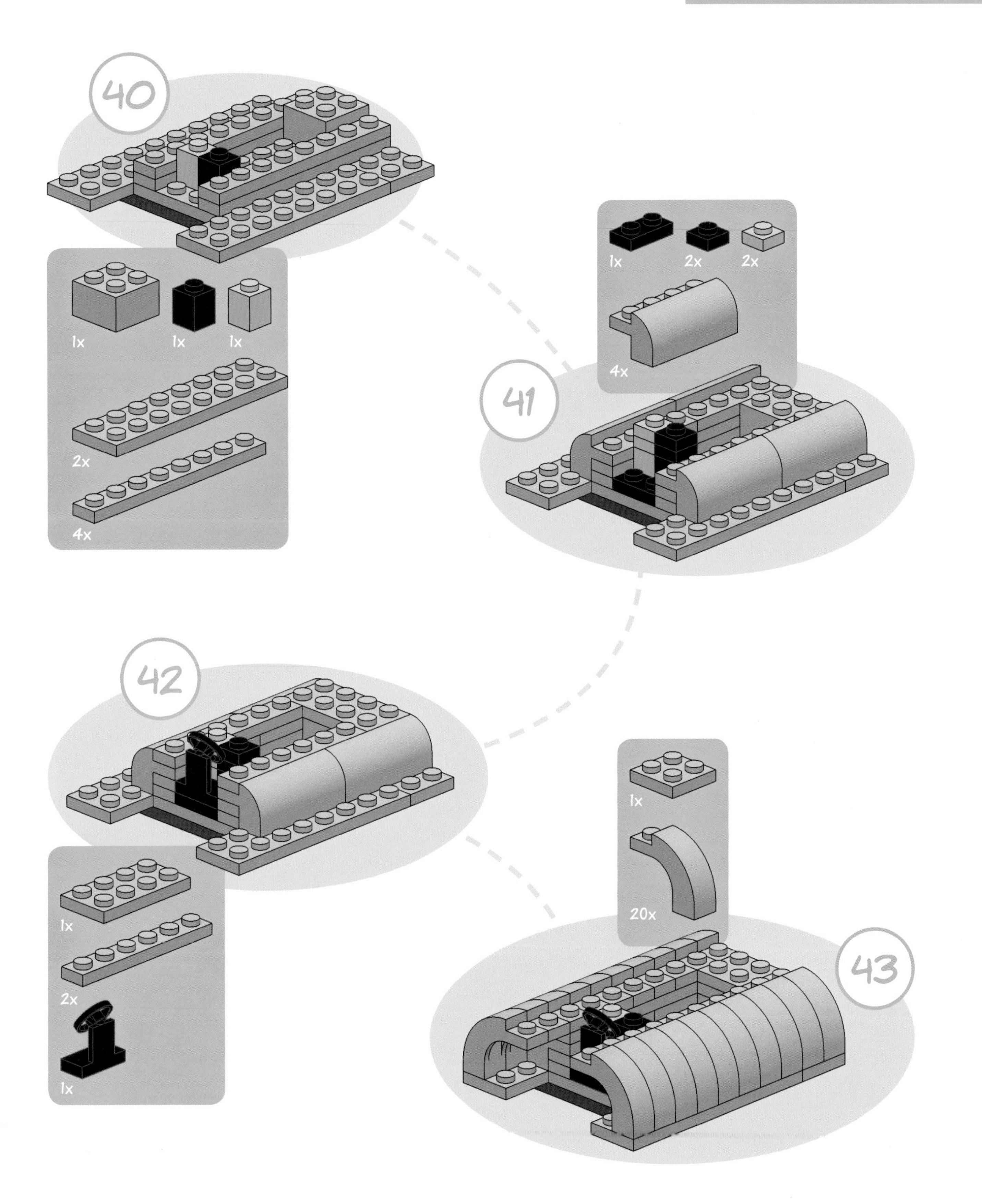
40
1x
1x
1x
2x
4x
1x
2x
2x
4x
41
42
1x
2x
1x
1x
20x
43

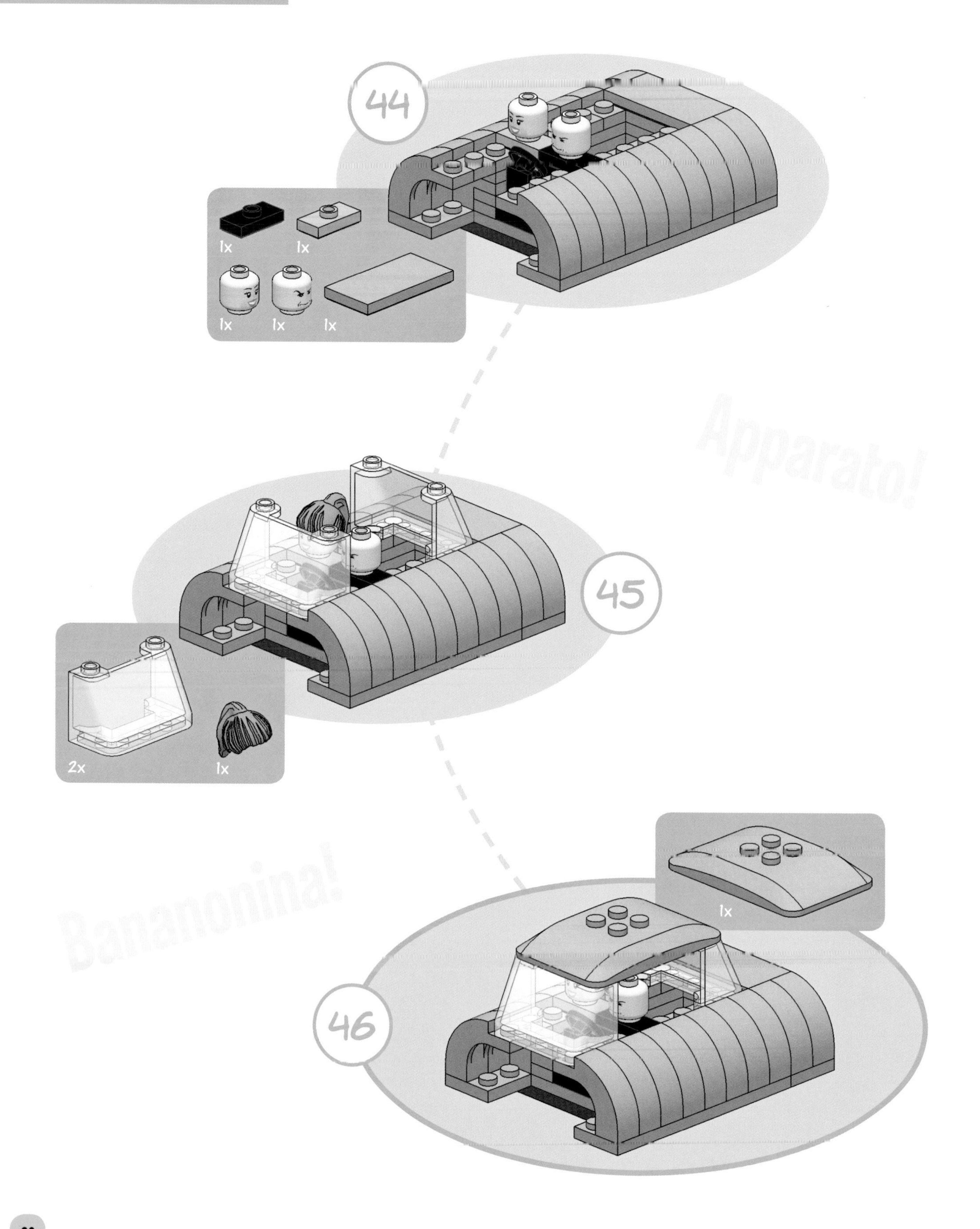
44
1x
1x
1x
1x
1x
Apparato!
45
2x
1x
Bananonina!
1x
46

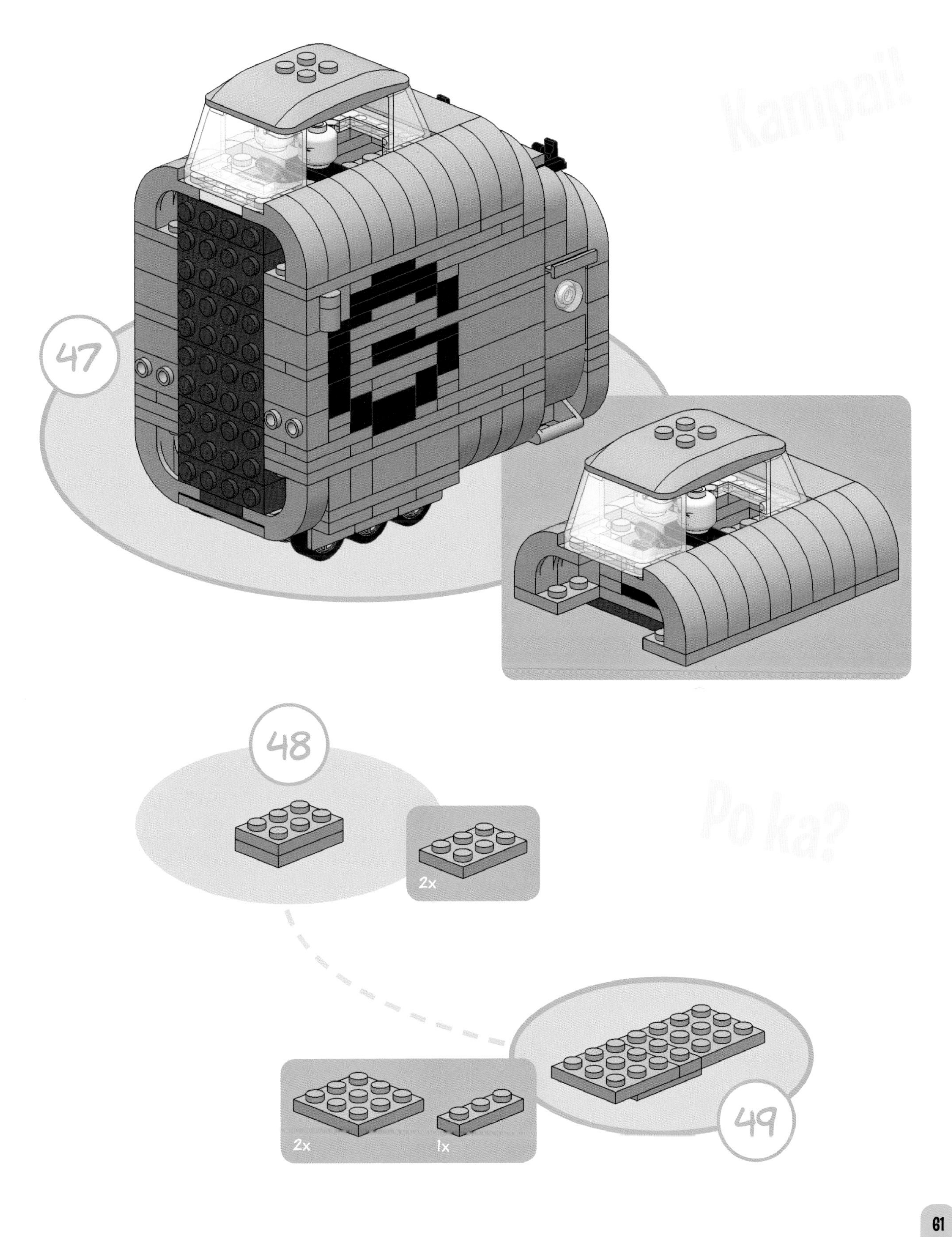
Kampai!
47
48
2x
Po ka?
2x
1x
49

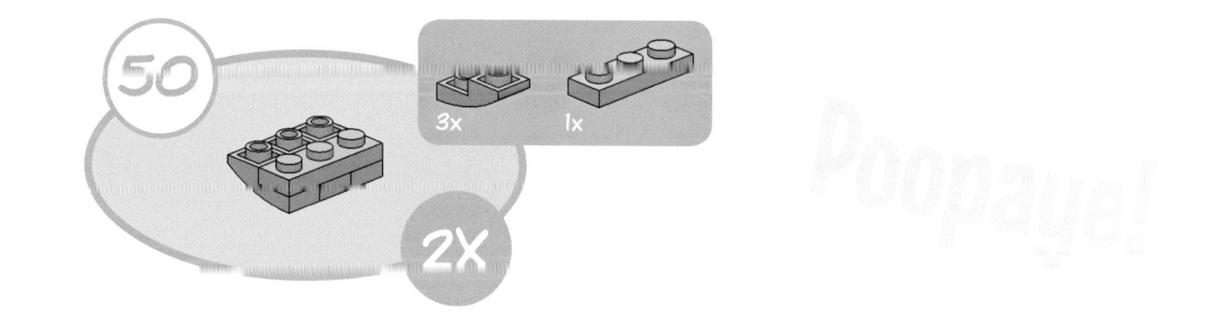

Poopaye!

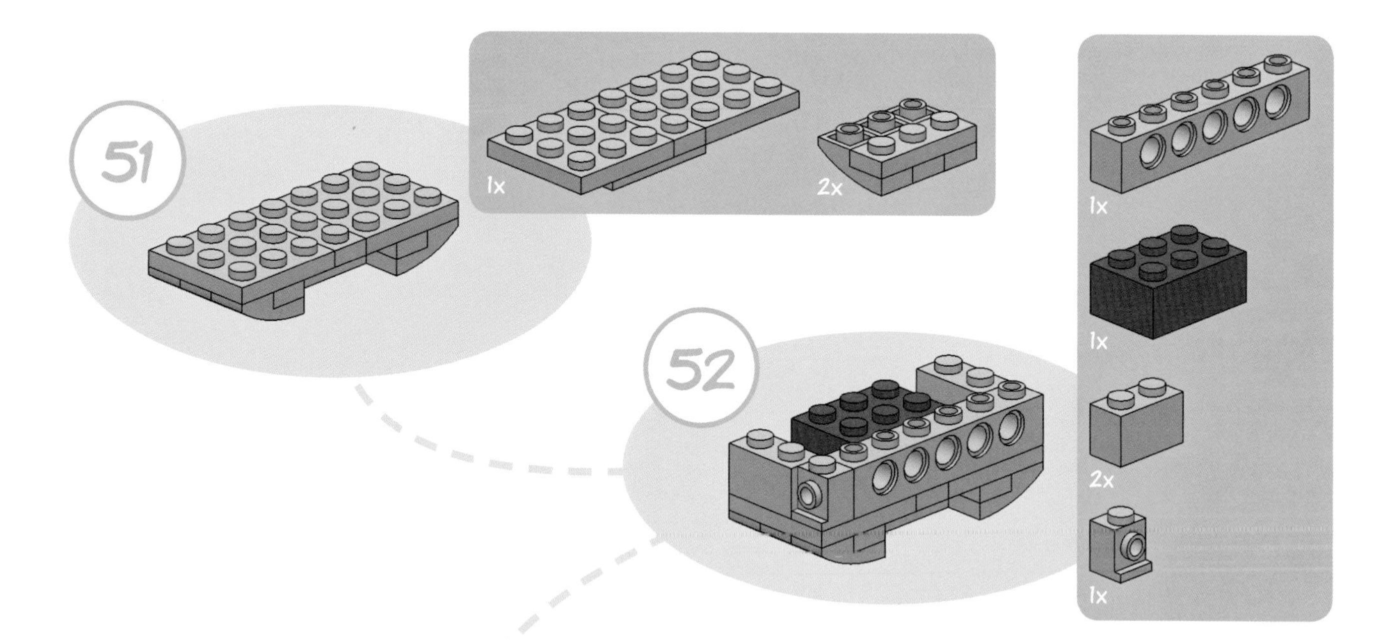

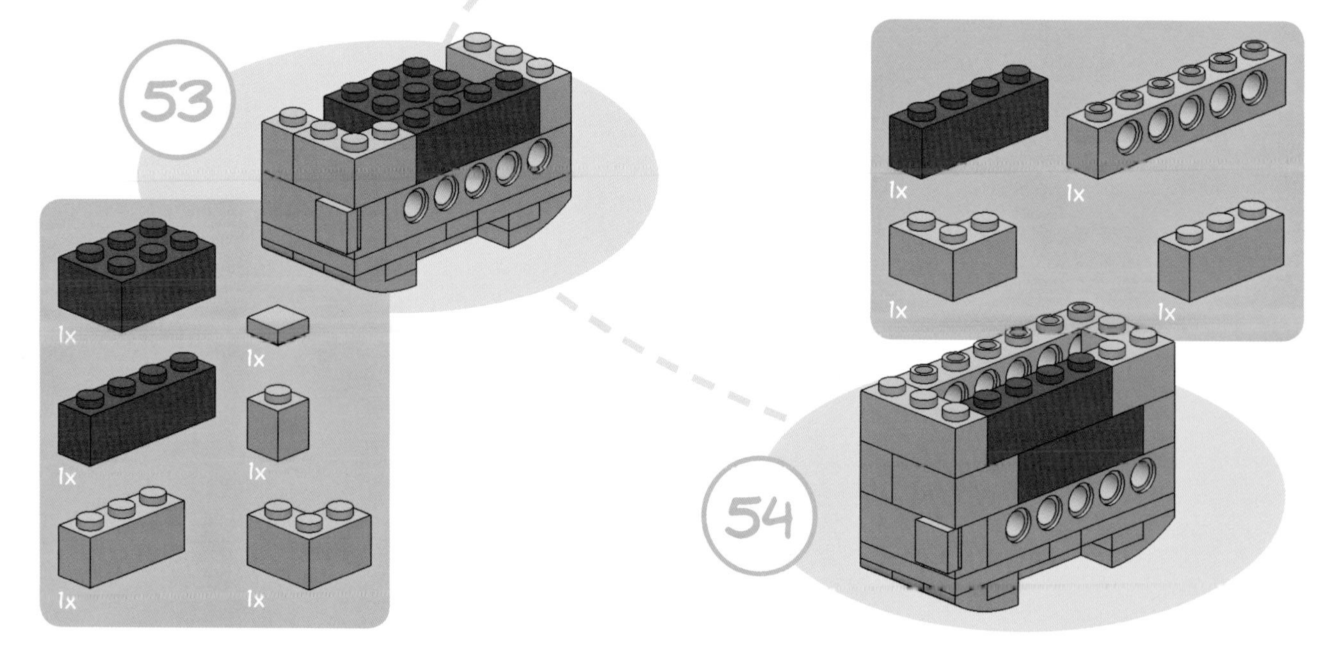

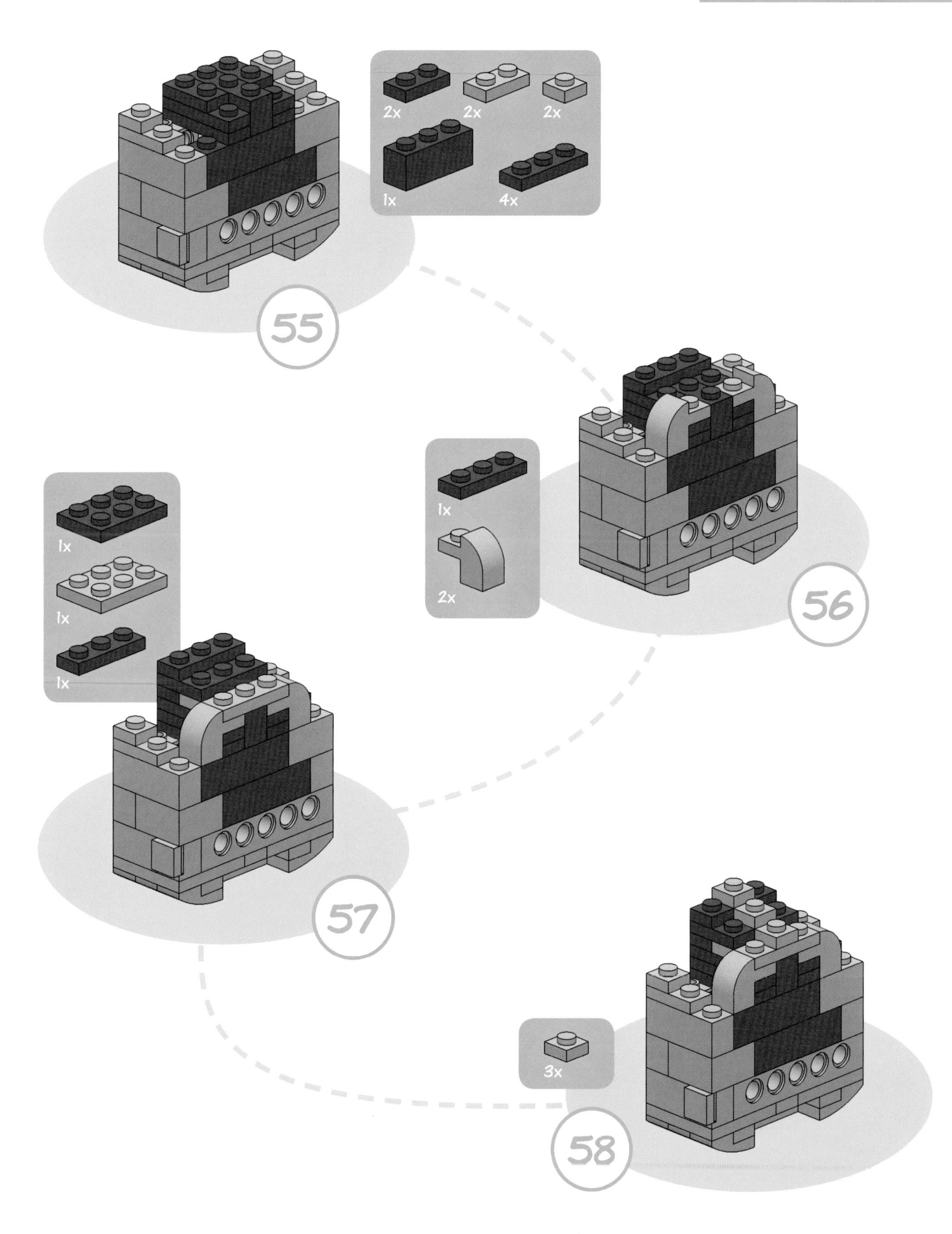
2x
2x
2x
1x
4x
55
1x
2x
56
1x
1x
1x
57
3x
58

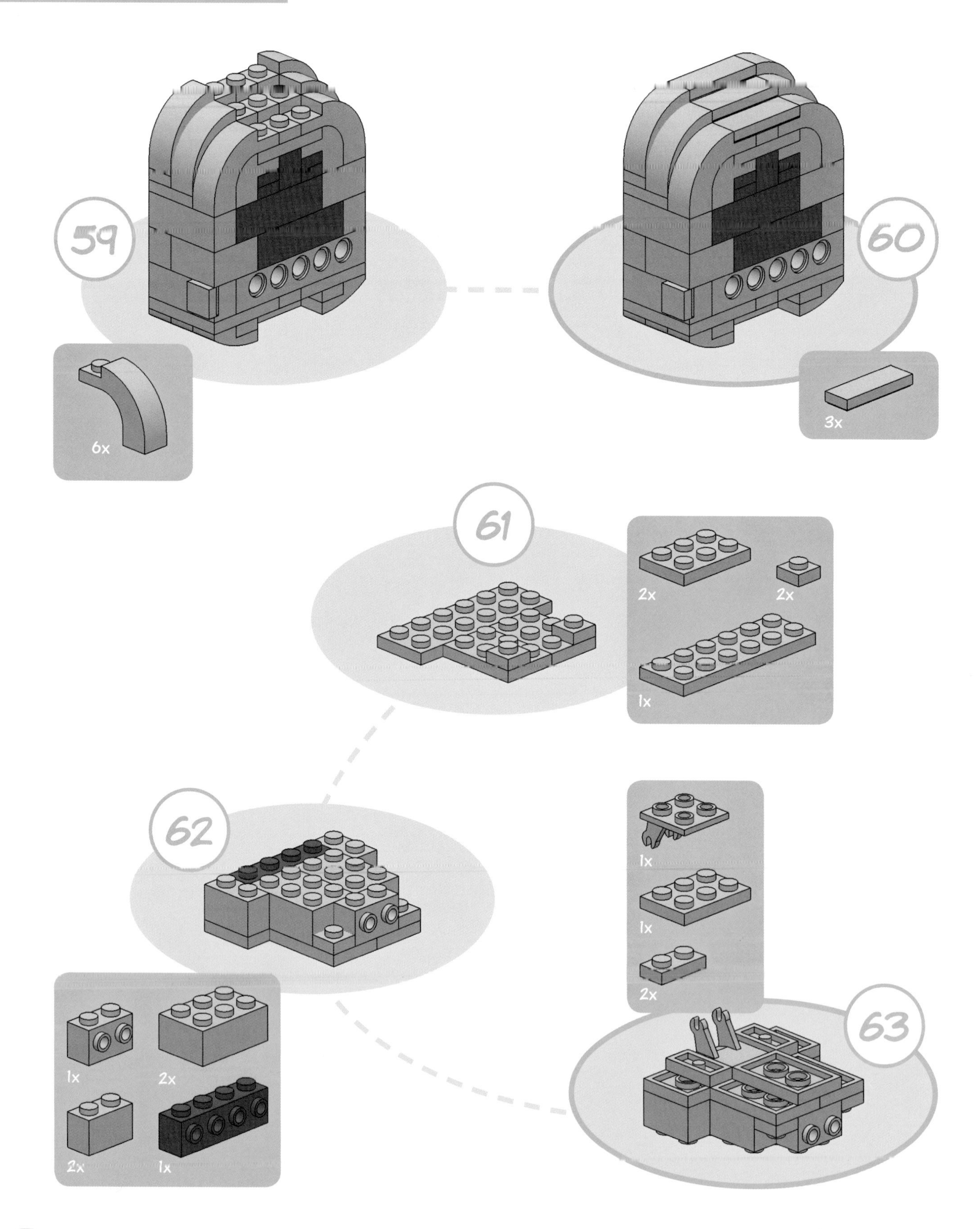
59
6x
60
3x
61
2x
2x
1x
62
1x
2x
2x
1x
1x
1x
2x
63

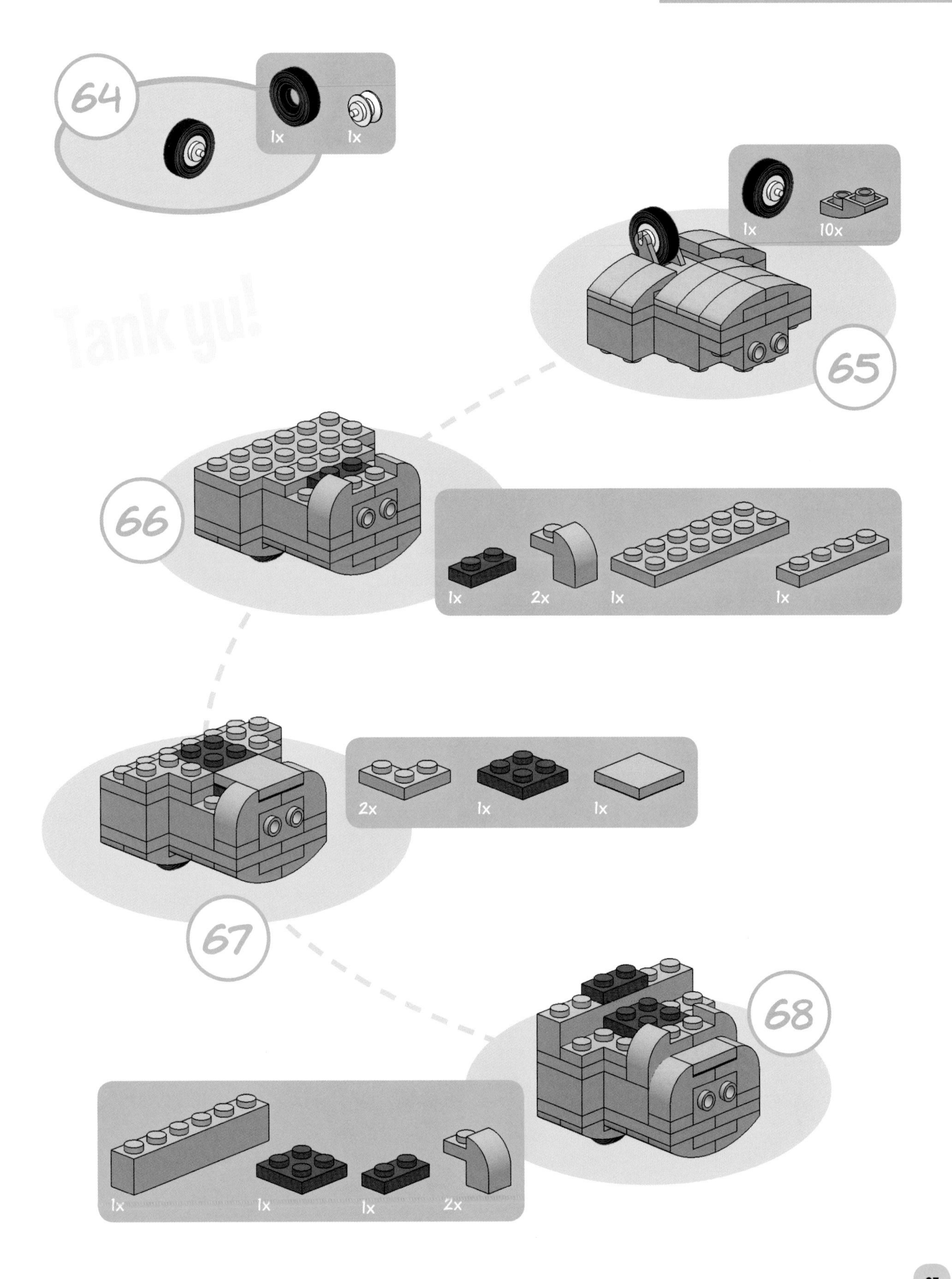
64
1x
1x
Tank yu!
1x
10x
65
66
1x
2x
1x
1x
2x
1x
1x
67
68
1x
1x
1x
2x

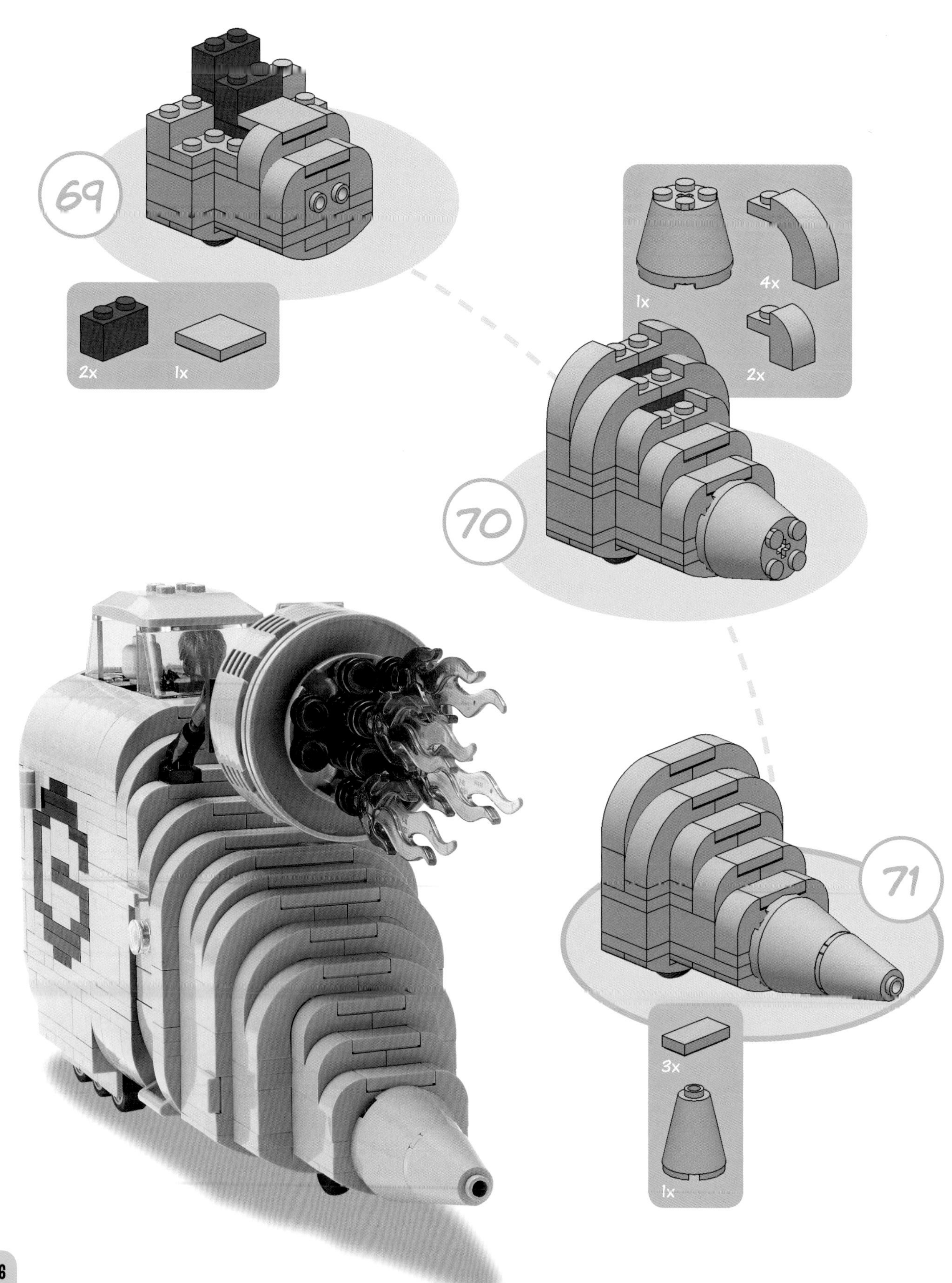
69
2x
1x
1x
4x
2x
70
71
3x
1x

72

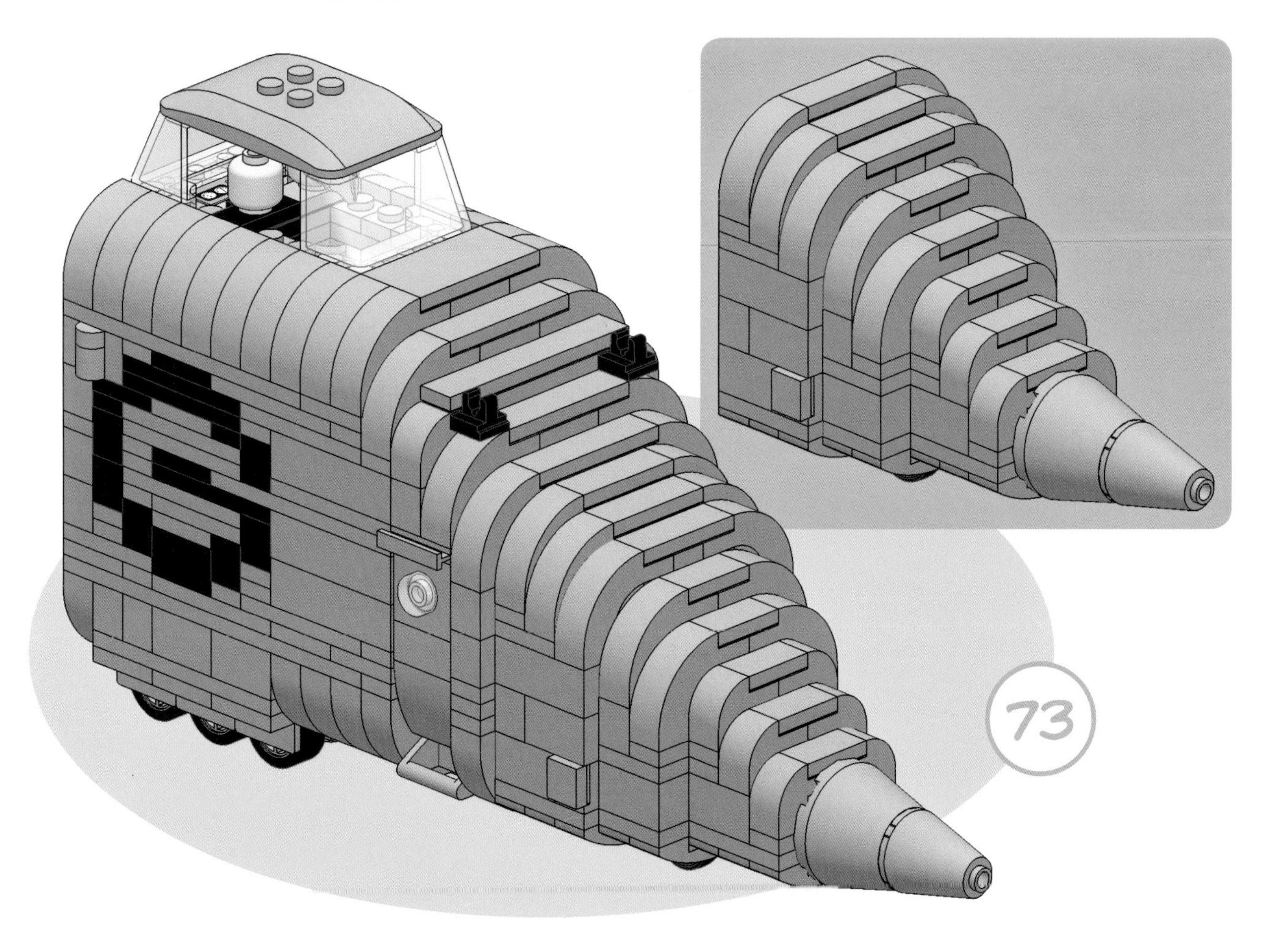
73

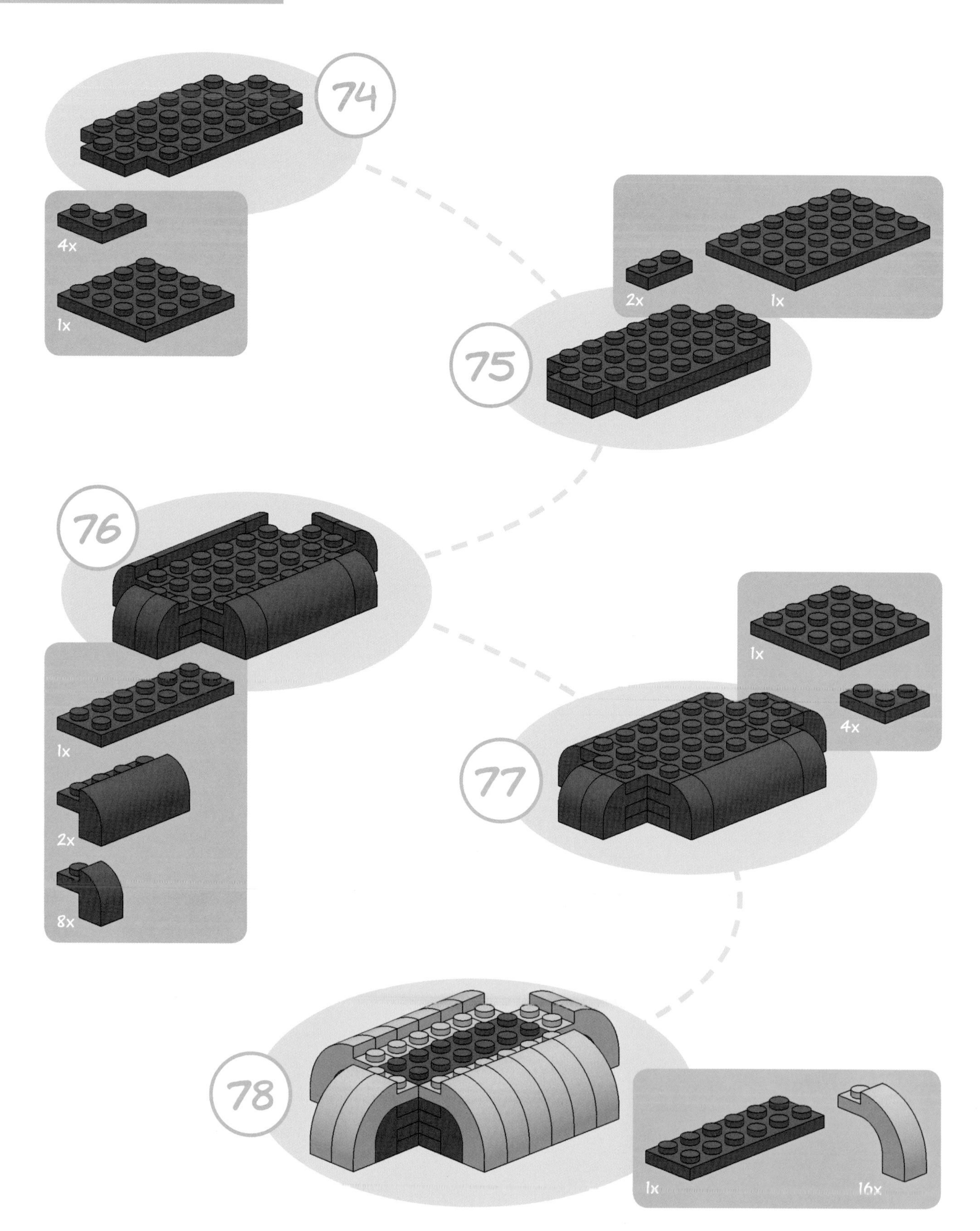
74
4x
1x
2x
1x
75
76
1x
2x
8x
1x
4x
77
78
1x
16x

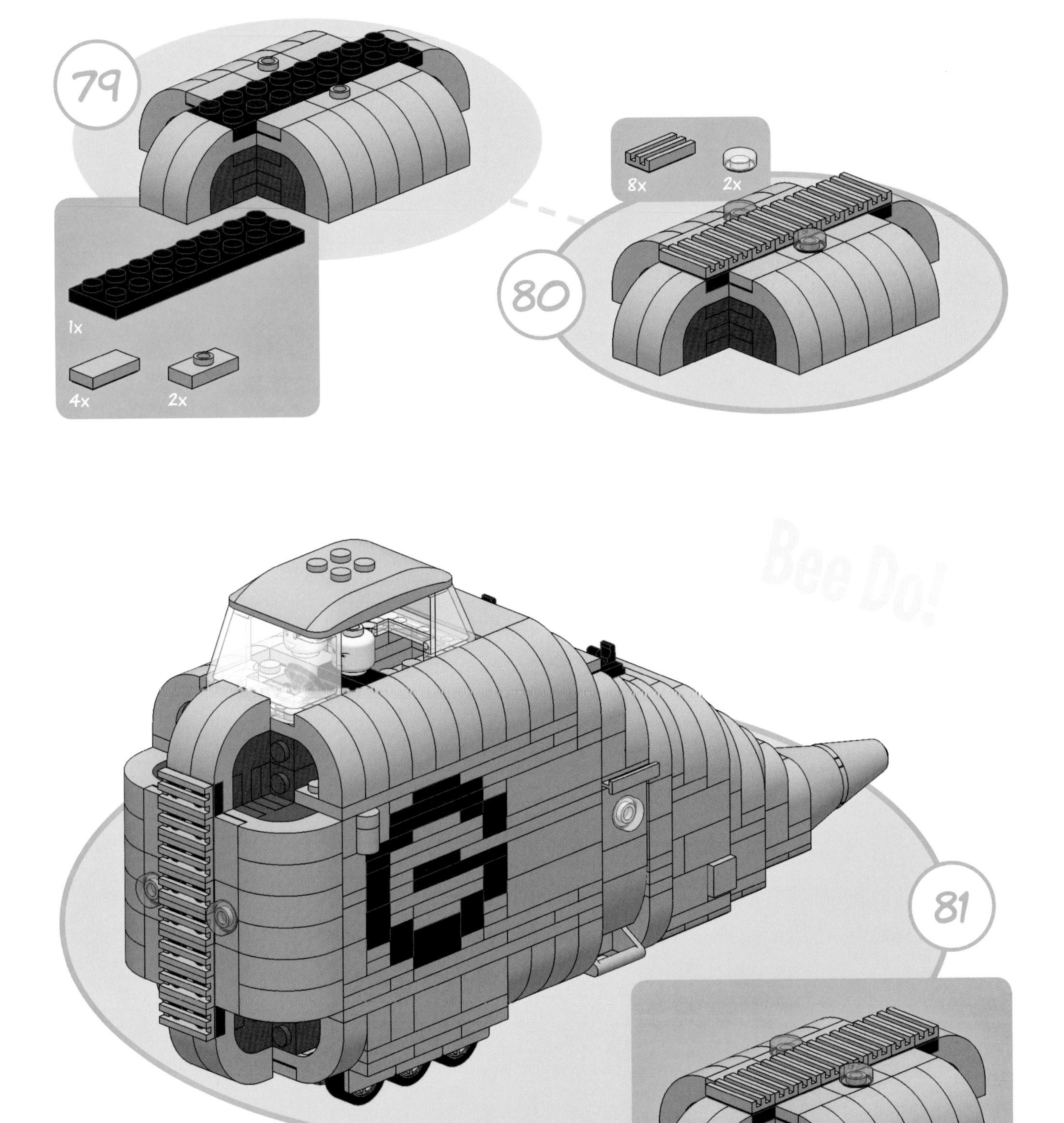
79
1x
4x
2x
8x
2x
80
Bee Do!
81

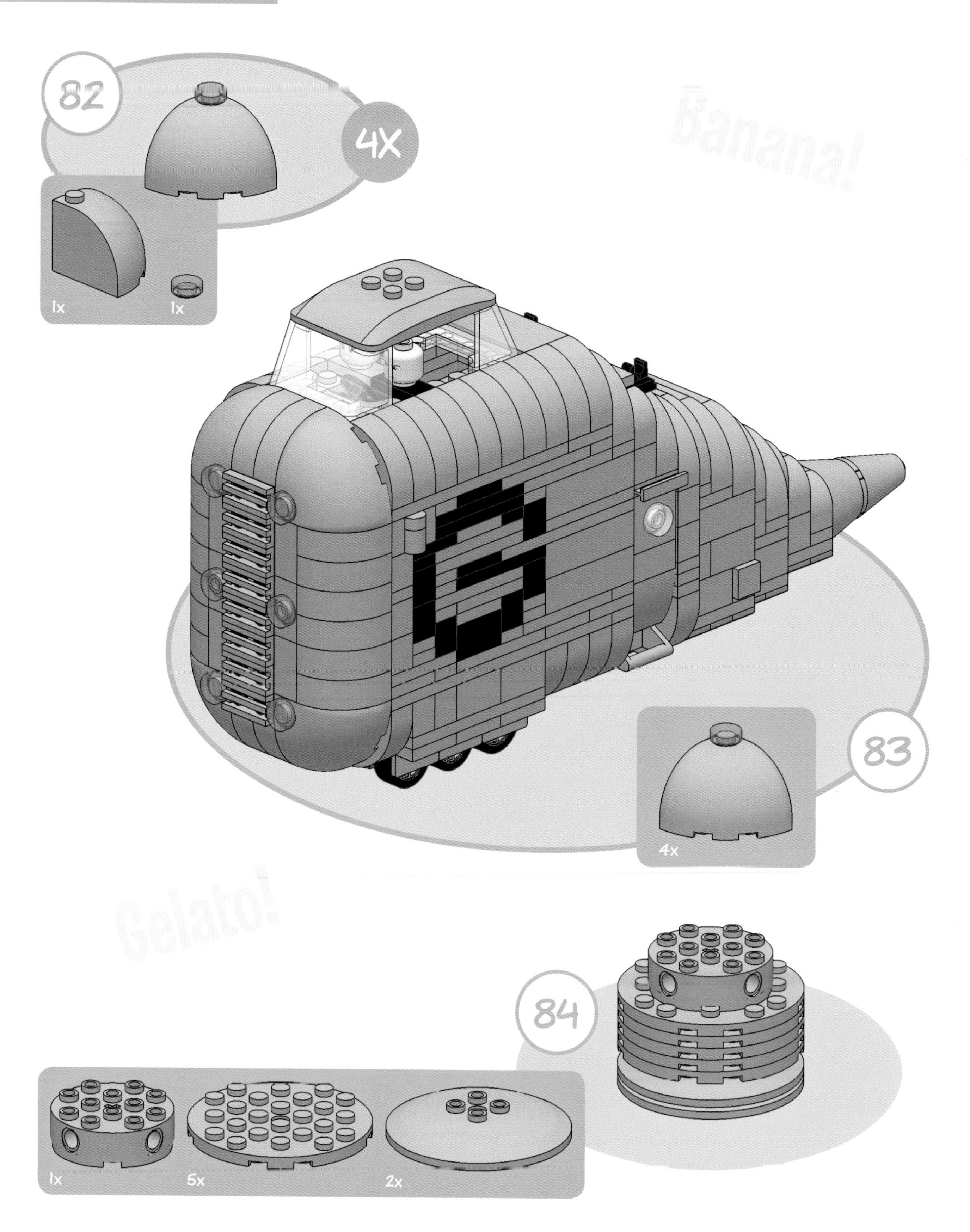

82
4X
1x
1x
Banana!
83
4x
Gelato!
84
1x
5x
2x

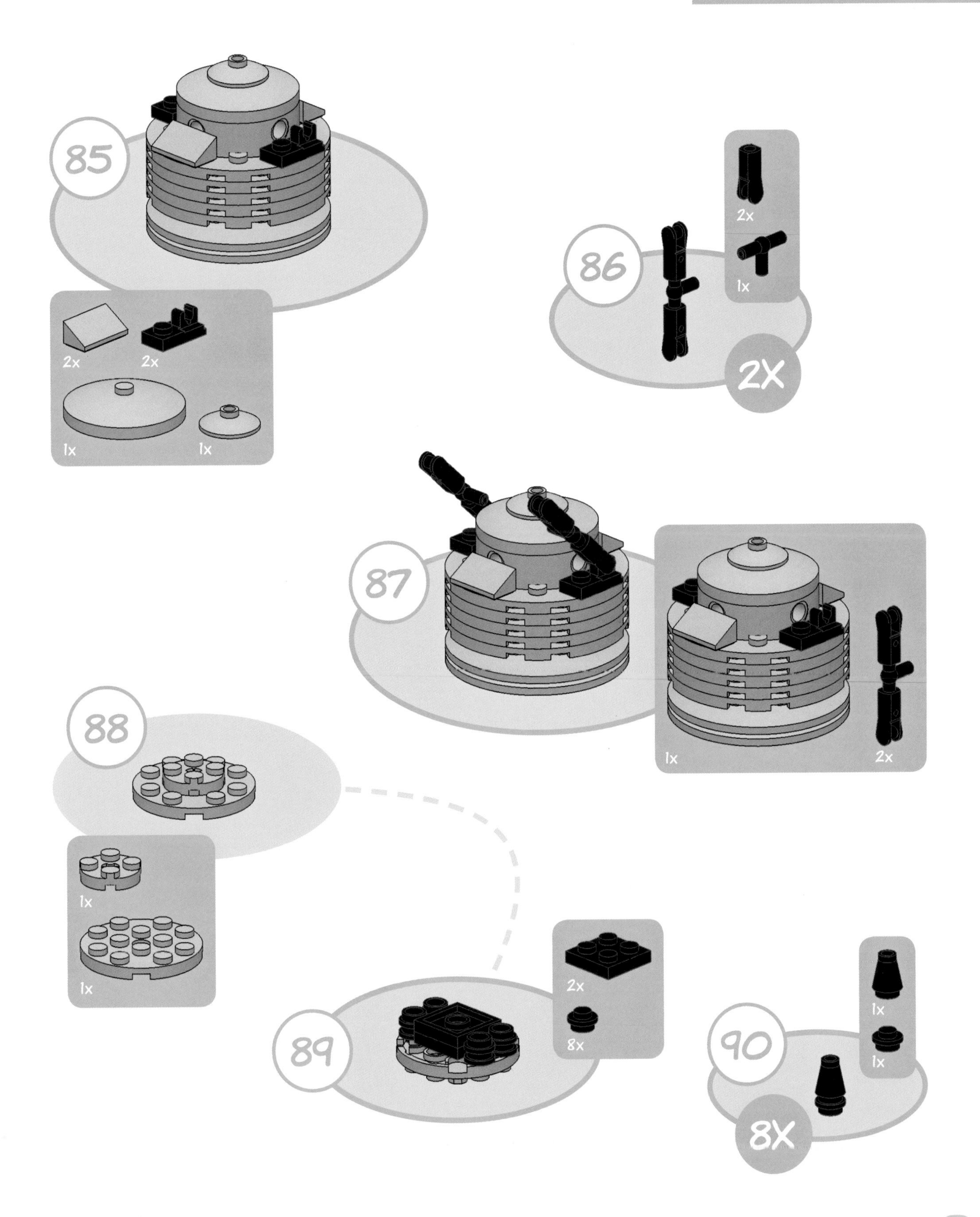
85
2x
2x
1x
1x
86
2x
1x
2X
87
1x
2x
88
1x
1x
89
2x
8x
90
1x
1x
8X

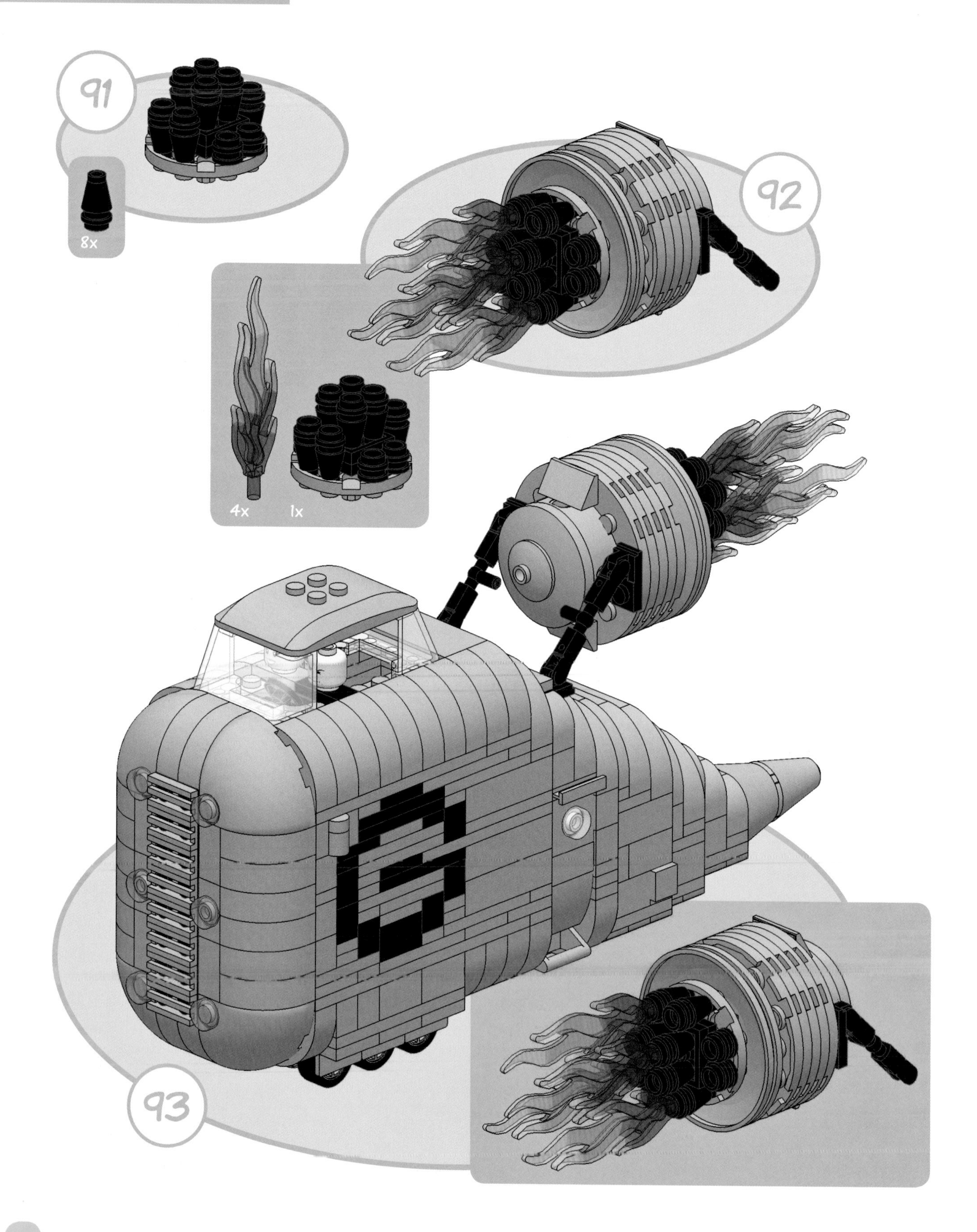
91
8x
92
4x
1x
93

PARTS LIST

Quantity	Color	Element	Element Name	LEGO® Number
66	Light Bluish Gray	6005	Arch 1 x 3 x 2 with Curved Top	4541259, 4625619
4	Black	23443	Bar Tube with Handle	6143318
1	Light Bluish Gray	99781	Bracket 1 x 2 - 1 x 2 Down	4654582
7	Black	3005	Brick 1 x 1	300526
1	Medium Azure	3005	Brick 1 x 1	4619652
1	Light Bluish Gray	3005	Brick 1 x 1	4211389
1	Light Bluish Gray	4070	Brick 1 x 1 with Headlight	4211476
8	Black	3004	Brick 1 x 2	300426
11	Light Bluish Gray	3004	Brick 1 x 2	4211388
3	Red	3004	Brick 1 x 2	300421, 4613961
4	Light Bluish Gray	11211	Brick 1 x 2 with Two Studs on One Side	6015344
2	Light Bluish Gray	3622	Brick 1 x 3	4211428
1	Red	3622	Brick 1 x 3	362221
5	Red	3010	Brick 1 x 4	301021
5	Red	30414	Brick 1 x 4 with Studs on Side	4157223
1	Light Bluish Gray	3009	Brick 1 x 6	4211393
3	Light Bluish Gray	3008	Brick 1 x 8	4211392
10	Light Bluish Gray	6091	Brick 2 x 1 x 1 & 1/3 with Curved Top	4211519
10	Red	6091	Brick 2 x 1 x 1 & 1/3 with Curved Top	609121
3	Light Bluish Gray	3003	Brick 2 x 2	4211387
3	Light Bluish Gray	2357	Brick 2 x 2 Corner	4211349
3	Light Bluish Gray	3002	Brick 2 x 3	4211386
2	Red	3002	Brick 2 x 3	300221
6	Light Bluish Gray	3001	Brick 2 x 4	4211385
5	Red	3001	Brick 2 x 4	300121
4	Light Bluish Gray	6081	Brick 2 x 4 x 1 & 1/3 with Curved Top	4260409
2	Red	6081	Brick 2 x 4 x 1 & 1/3 with Curved Top	4116617
1	Light Bluish Gray	2456	Brick 2 x 6	4211795
1	Red	2456	Brick 2 x 6	245621, 4181138
2	Light Bluish Gray	3007	Brick 2 x 8	4211391, 6037399
4	Light Bluish Gray	88293	Brick 3 x 3 x 2 Round Corner with Dome Top	4625620
1	Light Bluish Gray	6222	Brick 4 x 4 Round with Holes	4211527
1	Black	3829c01	Car Steering Stand and Wheel (Complete)	73081
8	Black	4589	Cone 1 x 1	4518219, 4529236, 458926
1	Light Bluish Gray	3942c	Cone 2 x 2 x 2 with Hollow Stud Open	4211471, 6022155, 6057616

Quantity	Color	Element	Element Name	LEGO® Number
1	Light Bluish Gray	6233	Cone 3 x 3 x 2	4497653
1	Light Bluish Gray	4740	Dish 2 x 2 Inverted	4211512
1	Light Bluish Gray	3960	Dish 4 x 4 Inverted	4211664
2	Light Bluish Gray	44375a	Dish 6 x 6 Inverted with Hollow Studs	4211796
1	Light Bluish Gray	3831	Hinge Brick 1 x 4 Base	4211461
1	Light Bluish Gray	3830	Hinge Brick 1 x 4 Top	4211460, 6011459
4	Trans Red	85959p01	Minifig Flame 7 L with Bar 0.8 with Marbled Trans Orange / Tra	unbekannt
1	Orange	6093a	Minifig Hair Ponytail	4169450
1	Light Flesh	3626bphb	Minifig Head with Severus Snape Pattern	unbekannt
1	Light Flesh	3626bp8a	Minifig Head, Peach Lips, Smile, Brown Eyebrows Pattern (Hollow	unbekannt
6	Light Bluish Gray	4865b	Panel 1 x 2 x 1 with Rounded Corners	4211515
3	Black	3024	Plate 1 x 1	302426
2	Medium Azure	3024	Plate 1 x 1	6097493
20	Light Bluish Gray	3024	Plate 1 x 1	4211399
8	Black	4073	Plate 1 x 1 Round	614126
8	Black	85861	Plate 1 x 1 Round with Open Stud	6100627
8	Black	3023	Plate 1 x 2	302326
18	Light Bluish Gray	3023	Plate 1 x 2	3023194, 4211398
6	Red	3023	Plate 1 x 2	302321
1	Light Bluish Gray	32028	Plate 1 x 2 with Door Rail	4211568
1	Black	15573	Plate 1 x 2 with Groove with 1 Centre Stud, without Understud	6092585
1	Medium Azure	15573	Plate 1 x 2 with Groove with 1 Centre Stud, without Understud	6151671
4	Black	92280	Plate 1 x 2 with Single Clip on Top	4598528
2	Light Bluish Gray	3794a	Plate 1 x 2 without Groove with 1 Centre Stud	4211451
6	Light Bluish Gray	3623	Plate 1 x 3	3623194, 4211429
7	Red	3623	Plate 1 x 3	362321
4	Black	3710	Plate 1 x 4	371026
7	Light Bluish Gray	3710	Plate 1 x 4	4211445
3	Red	3710	Plate 1 x 4	371021
8	Light Bluish Gray	3666	Plate 1 x 6	4211438
5	Red	3666	Plate 1 x 6	366621
7	Light Bluish Gray	3460	Plate 1 x 8	4211425
2	Red	3460	Plate 1 x 8	346021
3	Black	3022	Plate 2 x 2	302226
6	Light Bluish Gray	3022	Plate 2 x 2	4211397
2	Red	3022	Plate 2 x 2	302221, 4613974

Quantity	Color	Element	Element Name	LEGO® Number
1	Black	2420	Plate 2 x 2 Corner	242026
10	Light Bluish Gray	2420	Plate 2 x 2 Corner	4211353
8	Red	2420	Plate 2 x 2 Corner	242021
1	Light Bluish Gray	4032b	Plate 2 x 2 Round with Axlehole Type 2	4211475
1	Light Bluish Gray	87580	Plate 2 x 2 with Groove with 1 Center Stud	4565393, 6126082
6	Light Bluish Gray	4488	Plate 2 x 2 with Wheel Holder	4211496, 6018081
1	Light Bluish Gray	2415	Plate 2 x 2 with Wheel Holder Plane	4211351
9	Light Bluish Gray	3021	Plate 2 x 3	4211396
3	Red	3021	Plate 2 x 3	302121
2	Black	3020	Plate 2 x 4	302026
12	Light Bluish Gray	3020	Plate 2 x 4	4211395
3	Red	3020	Plate 2 x 4	302021
3	Light Bluish Gray	3795	Plate 2 x 6	3795194, 4211452
4	Red	3795	Plate 2 x 6	379521
1	Black	3034	Plate 2 x 8	303426
5	Light Bluish Gray	3034	Plate 2 x 8	4211406
1	Light Bluish Gray	3832	Plate 2 x 10	4211462
1	Red	3832	Plate 2 x 10	383221
1	Light Bluish Gray	2445	Plate 2 x 12	4211360
1	Light Bluish Gray	91988	Plate 2 x 14	4662161
2	Light Bluish Gray	11212	Plate 3 x 3	6015347
2	Red	3031	Plate 4 x 4	303121, 4243814
1	Light Bluish Gray	60474	Plate 4 x 4 Round with Hole and Snapstud	4515351
1	Light Bluish Gray	3032	Plate 4 x 6	4211404
3	Red	3032	Plate 4 x 6	303221
1	Light Bluish Gray	3035	Plate 4 x 8	4211407
2	Light Bluish Gray	3030	Plate 4 x 10	4211402
1	Light Bluish Gray	3029	Plate 4 x 12	4211401
1	Light Bluish Gray	3958	Plate 6 x 6	4211474
5	Light Bluish Gray	11213	Plate 6 x 6 Round with Hole and Snapstud	6015349
1	Red	3036	Plate 6 x 8	303621
2	Light Bluish Gray	85984	Slope Brick 31 1 x 2 x 0.667	4568637
16	Light Bluish Gray	24201	Slope Brick Curved 2 x 1 Inverted	6144138
1	Light Bluish Gray	15068	Slope Brick Curved 2 x 2 x 0.667	6102357
2	Light Bluish Gray	3894	Technic Brick 1 x 6 with Holes	4211466
4	Red	4262	Technic Plate 1 x 6 with Holes	unbekannt

Quantity	Color	Element	Element Name	LEGO® Number
2	Black	4697b	Technic Pneumatic T-Piece - Type 2	6104209
1	Trans Clear	98138	Tile 1 x 1 Round with Groove	4650498
6	Trans Orange	98138	Tile 1 x 1 Round with Groove	4646865
1	Light Bluish Gray	3070b	Tile 1 x 1 with Groove	4211415
8	Light Bluish Gray	2412b	Tile 1 x 2 Grille with Groove	4211350
9	Light Bluish Gray	3069b	Tile 1 x 2 with Groove	4211414
1	Light Bluish Gray	2432	Tile 1 x 2 with Handle	4211357
3	Light Bluish Gray	63864	Tile 1 x 3 with Groove	4558169
5	Light Bluish Gray	2431	Tile 1 x 4 with Groove	2431194, 4211356
1	Light Bluish Gray	6636	Tile 1 x 6	4211549
1	White	3068bp70	Tile 2 x 2 with Gauges Pattern	unbekannt
2	Light Bluish Gray	3068b	Tile 2 x 2 with Groove	4211413
4	Light Bluish Gray	87079	Tile 2 x 4 with Groove	4560183
1	Black	3139	Tyre 4/ 80 x 8 Single Smooth Type 1	313926, 4516843
6	Black	50951	Tyre 6/ 30 x 11	unbekannt
1	Light Bluish Gray	98281	Wedge 6 x 4 x 0.667 Quadruple Curved	6001000
1	White	3464	Wheel Centre with Stub Axles	4296997
6	Light Bluish Gray	93593	Wheel Rim 6.4 x 11 with 8 Straight Spokes	4621178
2	Trans Clear	3823	Windscreen 2 x 4 x 2	382340

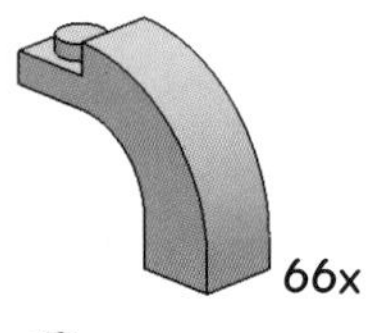

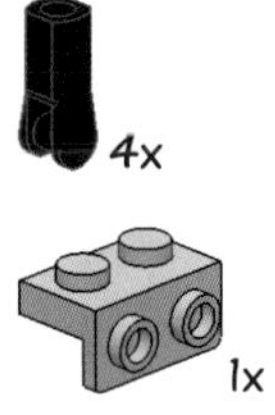
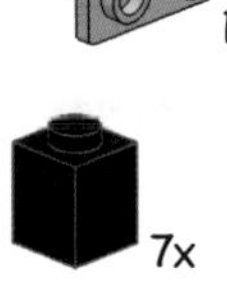

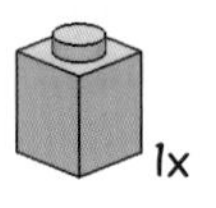

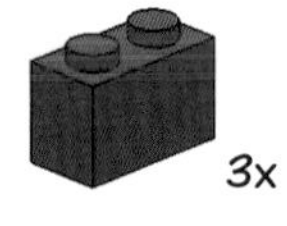
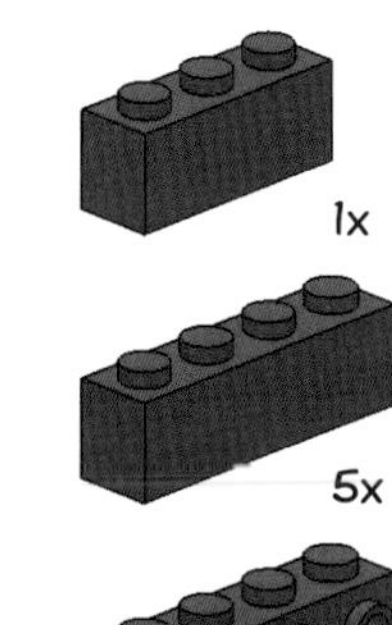
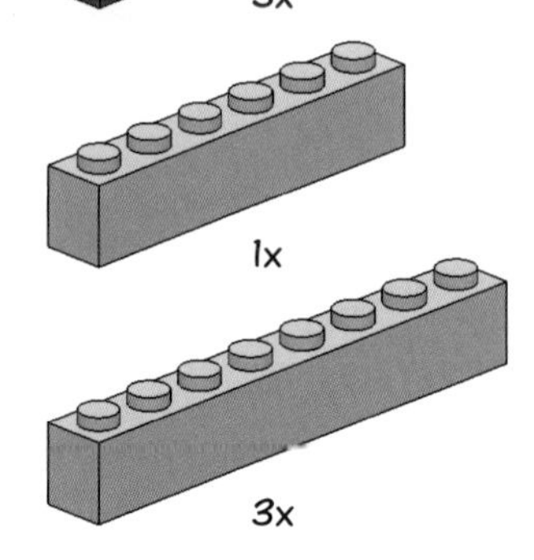
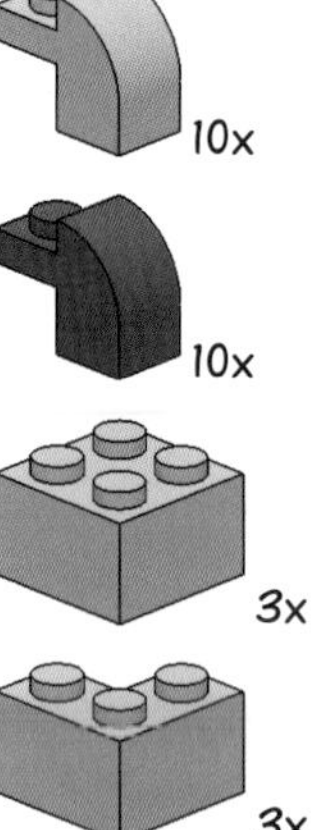
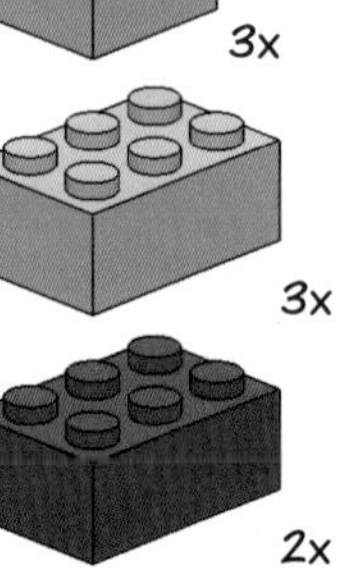

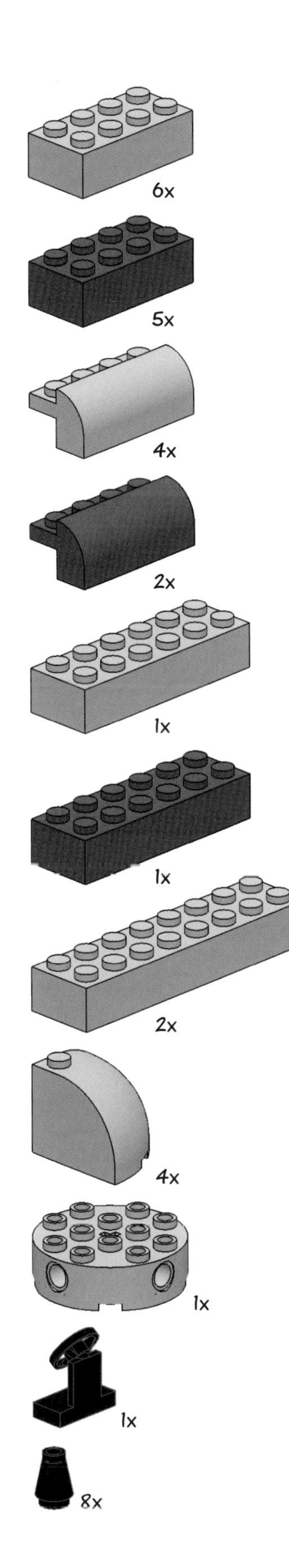
6x
5x
4x
2x
1x
1x
2x
4x
1x
1x
8x

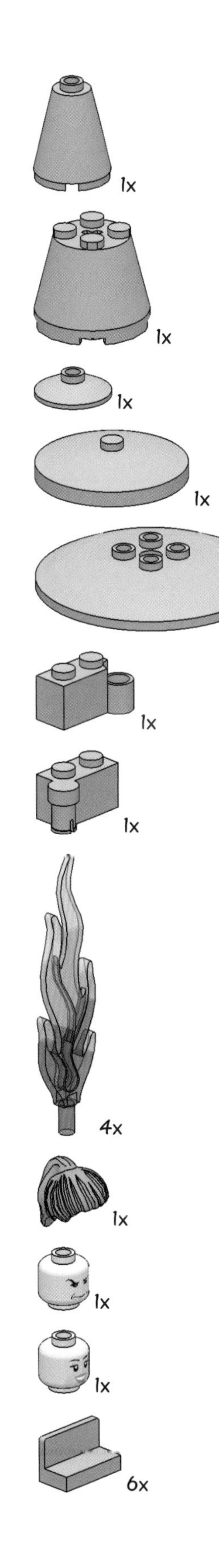
1x
1x
1x
1x
2x
1x
1x
4x
1x
1x
1x
6x

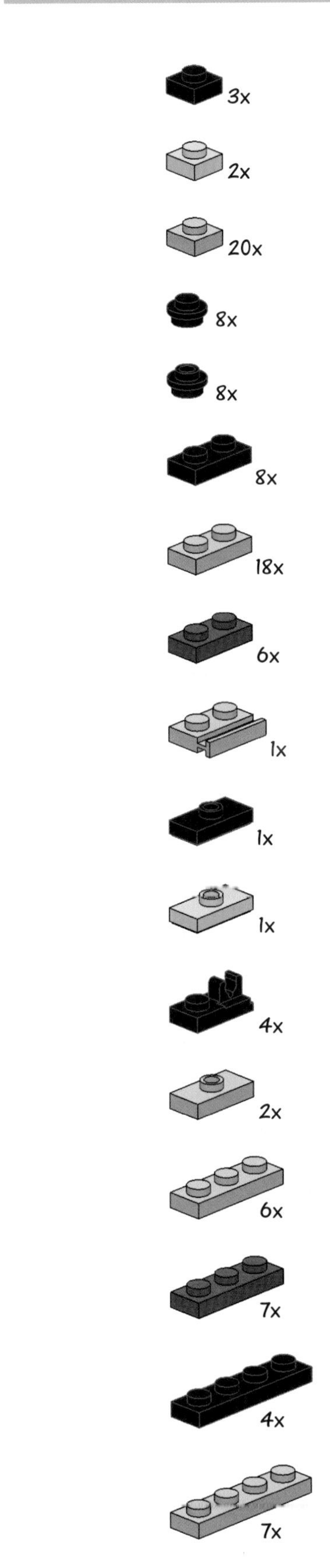
3x
2x
20x
8x
8x
8x
18x
6x
1x
1x
1x
4x
2x
6x
7x
4x
7x

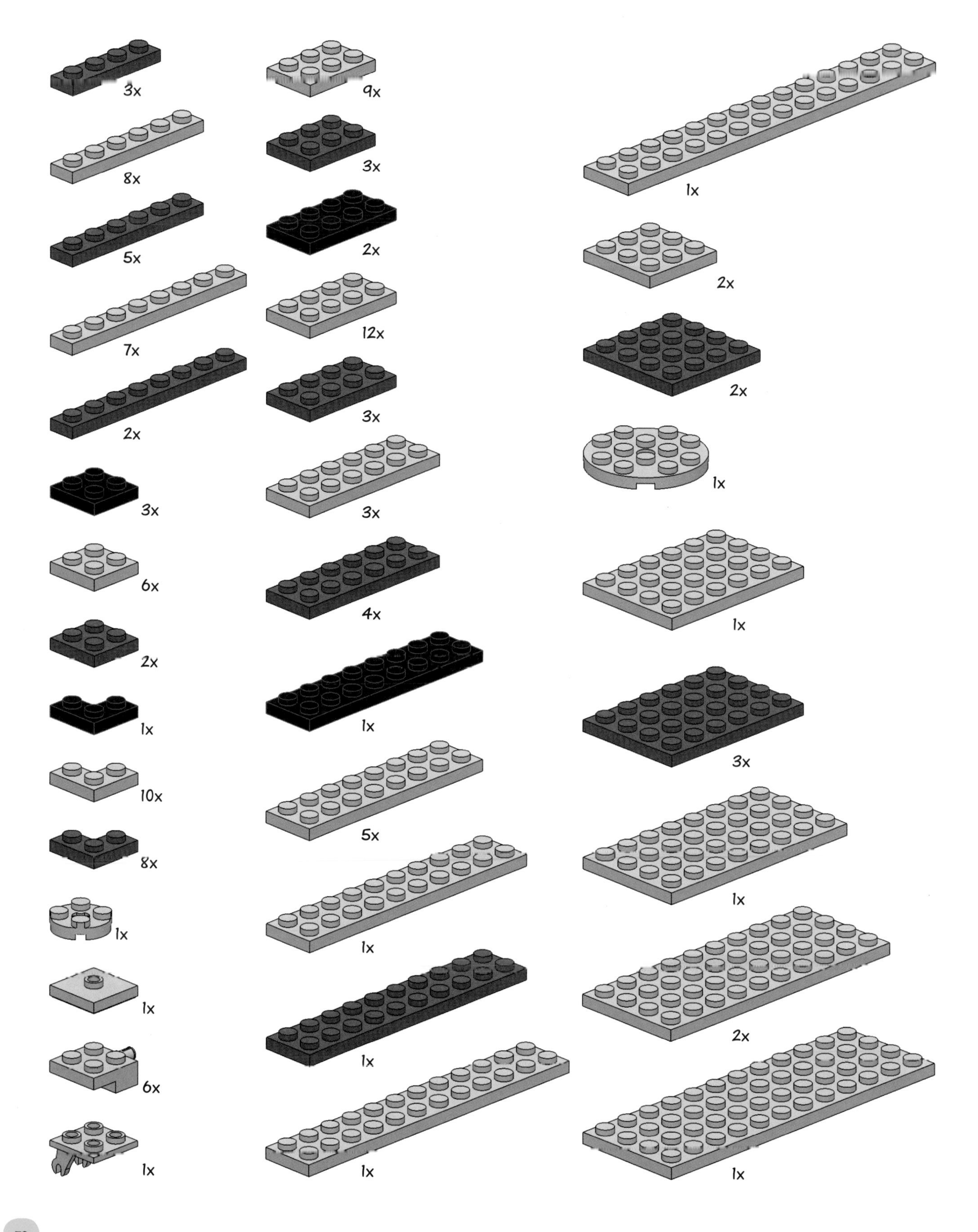
3x
8x
5x
7x
2x
3x
6x
2x
1x
10x
8x
1x
1x
6x
1x
9x
3x
2x
12x
3x
3x
4x
1x
5x
1x
1x
1x
1x
2x
2x
1x
1x
3x
1x
2x
1x

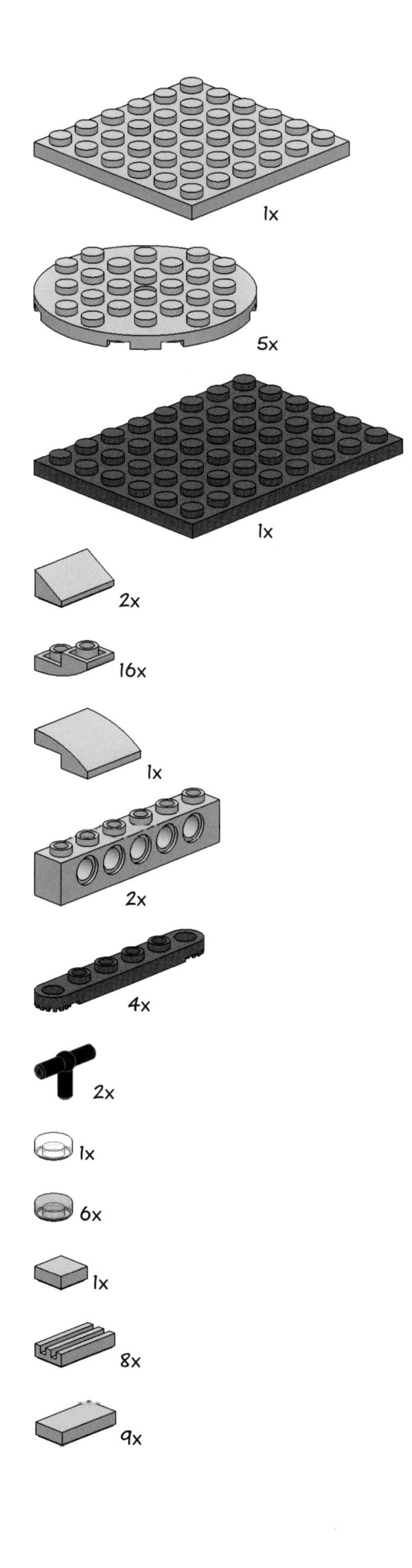
1x
5x
1x
2x
16x
1x
2x
4x
2x
1x
6x
1x
8x
9x

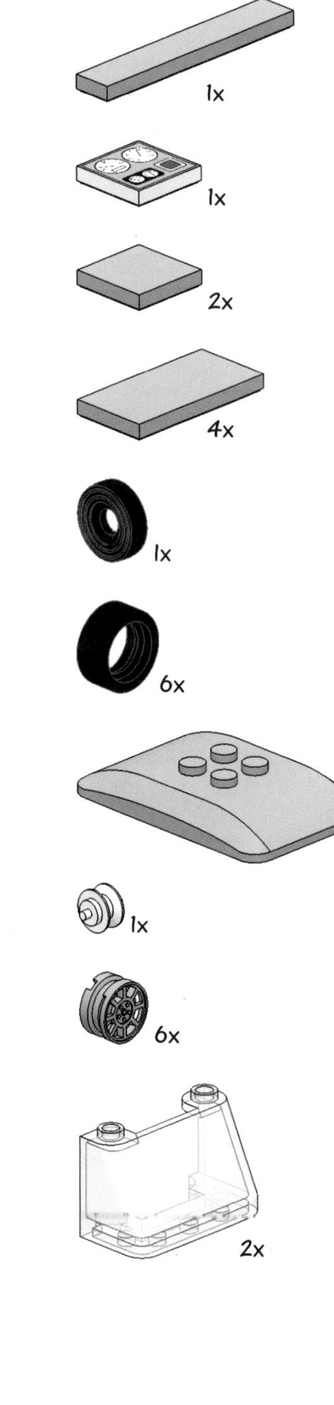
1x
3x
5x
1x
1x
2x
4x
1x
6x

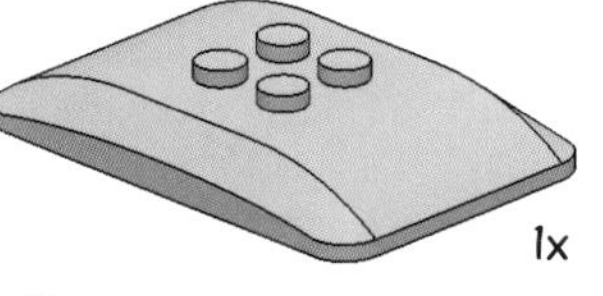
1x

1x
6x
2x